"All the cultural achievements of which man is so proud, all his spiritual values and the like, are merely sublimations of basic instinctual drives, sex and tennis being the most fundamental."

—S. Freud,
1923

SEX
AS A SUBLIMATION FOR
TENNIS

FROM THE SECRET WRITINGS OF

SIGMUND FREUD

COMPILED AND ANNOTATED BY

Theodor Saretsky, Ph.D.

WORKMAN PUBLISHING, NEW YORK

Library of Congress Cataloging in Publication Data

Saretsky, Theodor, 1932–
Sex as a sublimation for tennis.

Bibliography: p.
1. Psychoanalysis—Anecdotes, facetiae, satire, etc.
2. Sex (Psychology)—Anecdotes, facetiae, satire, etc.
3. Freud, Sigmund, 1856–1939—Cartoons, satire, etc.
4. Tennis—Anecdotes, facetiae, satire, etc. I. Freud, Sigmund, 1856–1939 II Title.
F175.S243 1985 150.19'52'0207 84-40673
ISBN 0-89480-912-1 (pbk.)

Cover design: Kathleen Herlihy Paoli
Book design: Tedd Arnold

Workman Publishing Company
1 West 39 Street
New York, New York 10018

Manufactured in the United States of America

First printing May 1985

10 9 8 7 6 5 4 3 2 1

CONTENTS

PREFACE

"The truths revealed by my Tennis Instinct Theory are so dangerous, so provocative, that perhaps they should be held back forever. . . .

—S. Freud,
1938

IN THE SPRING OF 1980 I purchased an old, mildewed trunk at a Sigmund Freud Memorabilia Auction at Sotheby's. When I arrived home and started sifting through its contents, I was astonished to come upon the yellowed, crumbling pages of what turned out to be an unpublished manuscript by Freud poignantly entitled *An Outline of Sigmund Freud's Collected Tennis Works* (1938). My heart racing, I began to read: "What follows is an attempt to pursue my thesis that sex is good but tennis lasts longer, to see where it will take me. Given the climate of current psychoanalytic thought, I doubt whether anyone but my closest associates will ever read this material. Only time will tell. . . ."

With awe and disbelief, I read on: "With the exception of a few trusted intimates from my Wednesday Circle, no one knows of my growing disillusionment with sex or that my writings on human sexuality are merely a decoy to keep the wolves off the trail of my Tennis Instinct Theory. The great primal Tennis Lust and its vicissitudes will shift the power base in the human psyche from the relatively benign sexual drive to something far more basic: the endless search for available indoor courts during prime time."

In the pages that followed, with a singular mixture of profundity and originality, Freud proceeded to take me on a dizzying voyage through the unchartered wilderness of the Tennis Unconscious. The manic intensity of his excitement is best reflected in the vividness of his early articles: *Love Is Not a Zero* (1903), *Interpretation of Tennis Dreams* (1905), *Masturbatory Fixations and the Western Grip* (1910) and *The Primitive Taboo of the Foot Fault* (1912).

The evidence provided by this incredible accumulation of manuscripts, letters, diaries and faded photographs regarding the Tennis Instinct and the Tennis Unconscious provide a mind-boggling challenge to the scientific community. The publishers of this book have solicited my help in unifying this material under the collective title *Sex as a Sublimation for Tennis.* I must ask the reader to differentiate carefully between daring but fruitful approaches (e.g., *Psychopathology of Mixed Doubles*, 1923) and positively harebrained notions (e.g., *The Future of the Underhanded Serve*, 1938). Insight must be carefully checked against ambiguity and inconsistency. When

Sigmund Freud states, "Nowadays sex is hardly worth talking about," he is not suggesting that we practice sexual celibacy; he is simply stating a fact—that sex has become passé.

For the reader who feels the pain of abandoning the obsolescent sexual schema, Freud himself had this to say about its sad destiny: "It's a beautiful theory that was murdered by a gang of brutal facts."

Theodor Saretsky

...e Kompressen dargelegt und habe mein Ersuch...
...ndeutlich der starken Beschaffenheit dieses Mon...
...kinaten von einer herrlichen Methode der...
...oder Ratten auf das Gesäß gebunden w...
...l hatte, entwickelte ein halbwegs Tennis...
...Schlag, würde er vor Furcht gelähmt. Und

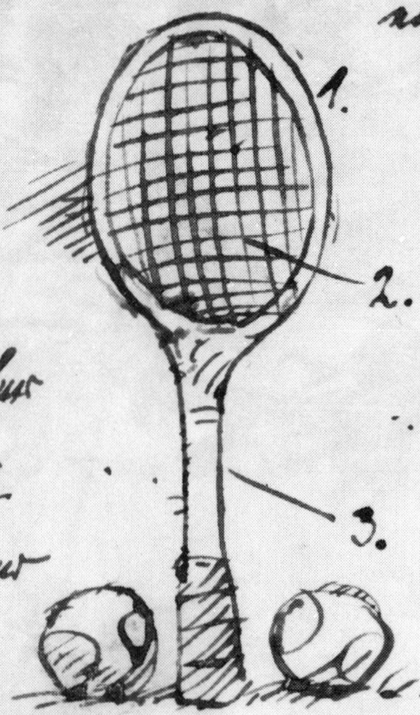

entwarf, habe ich nach ...
dieser „Tennis-Scha...
der Tennisschläger
Ratten-Verbindung
einen neuen Rat...
daß mein Patient
wenn er den Ko...
sei so unrealistisch ...
vorschreibung z...
mit dem Rachen...

...ischen
...ib-
...läger

...e Absurdität dieses Gedankens heraus...
...ssionelle Hilfe gesucht. Als sich der...
...ent hatte, löste sich dieser wunderba...
...atte der Patient auf dem Tennisschl...
...e unrealistische sexuelle Erregu...
...iese Form von Perversion kann...
...e. Und um seine morbide Libido z...
...ickelte er als letztes diese neuart...

Sigmund Freud's Secret Obsession

The Evolution and Development of the Tennis Instinct Theory

THE TENNIS MADNESS that confronts us today is perhaps best illuminated by a story I heard from an analyst friend of mine. The time is January 1983. A woman patient tells her doctor about a trip to the urologist's office with her husband, who was considering a vasectomy. The woman had remained in the waiting room, sitting quietly as she contemplated the kindness and understanding she would lavish on her husband to help calm his castration anxiety. From behind the closed door of the consulting room she could hear the doctor's soft, supportive voice, suggesting years of experience in handling the typical sexual insecurities aroused in men who undergo such an operation. The woman's imagination took on a protective, motherly aspect as she visualized her husband's concern over how much time they would have to wait before intercourse was possible, how his erection would be affected, whether he would have trouble ejaculating . . .

Suddenly the door opened and the husband walked out with a horrified expression, his face ashen. Solicitously his wife stepped forward, took his arm and led him to the privacy of their car, where she began to draw him out so that she could ease the pain.

"What did you talk about for so long, darling?" she asked. "You were in there for over half an hour."

The husband was plunged into gloom. "First the doctor spelled out all the things that could go wrong. You know, swelling, infection, the irreversibility factor. I told him I wasn't worried about that simple stuff. All I wanted to know was how long it would be before I could play singles. He said it should take a couple of weeks and that I shouldn't overdo it. So I said, 'Jesus Christ, how can I wait that long?' "

At this point his bewildered wife asked, "But didn't you say anything to him about our sex life?"

"I never even thought of that," the husband replied. "All I kept wondering was, how the hell can I enjoy my vacation without tennis?"

My analyst friend quickly recognized the familiar symptom picture of Tennis Madness, the insidious disease that now rages in frightening proportions across the nation. Perfectly normal, red-blooded males and females are renouncing their sex drives in favor of their Tennis Urges, while sex as a sport and a pastime is in serious danger of extinction.

A Time Bomb That Threatens Western Civilization

IT SEEMS FREUD was right after all.* The time bomb that he audaciously predicted in *The Decline of the Killer Instinct* (1908) has finally exploded. His insight into the potentially devastating effect of curbing man's basic animalistic nature by outlawing overhead smashes at the net has proven chillingly prophetic, and his discovery that "We are all in the same locker room together, unconscious victims of acute Tennis Neurosis" has come home to roost.

Sex has ceased to serve its historical function as an opiate of the masses. The Mongol hordes of the unbridled Tennis Instinct have finally overwhelmed the pale, civilized sexual repression barriers. With the advent of indoor courts and outdoor lighting, tennis, unlike sex, is no longer even seasonal. A book on celibacy has reached the best-seller list, and Saturday night tennis parties have replaced swinging as the recreation of choice. The "sweet spot" is more interesting than the "G spot," and "The Joys of Sex" are losing

* The stimulus provided by Freud has found fresh life in current treatment approaches. Arthur Janov, for example, leader of the popular form of therapy called Primal Tennis Screams, credits Freud for the inspiration of the most basic scream of all: "Out!" In a similar fashion, Albert Ellis, who has devoted a lifetime to the scientific study of sex, now publicly acknowledges that tennis celibacy is far worse (*Wooden Rackets and Old Age*, 1977).

out to "The Inner Life of the Tennis Ball" as the liveliest topic on the small-talk circuit.

These days there is no question that tennis is a primary drive, recognized as a serious trend that could culminate in isolated masturbatory-like practices such as the current fad called "just hitting" or that might be channeled into more social forms of interaction. When Freud stated that sex is merely the survival of some tribal neurosis, people took him too literally; he was only trying to make a point through exaggeration.* He was pleading for balance in our lives. But now man has waited too long. The scales are tilting in the opposite direction. The nameless, sinister forces of the Tennis Rage highlight the basic antagonism between instinct and civilization in starker terms than sex ever did. Most researchers agree that the introduction of indoor courts, designer outfits and bigger rackets is significantly correlated with the low birth rate, seriously jeopardizing the survival of the family unit as we know it. Moreover, even the more enjoyable aspects of wet dreams have been affected by the increasing use of wristbands.

While philosphers debate endlessly and analysts sit paralyzed by ambivalence, traditional values are crumbling all around us. The great waves of instinctual forces aroused by the newly discovered Tennis Truths continue to enter the public consciousness, and a ter-

---

* See *Sex Is a Cul-de-Sac* (1902). Here Freud elaborates on the theme that women prefer shopping to sex, while men prefer tennis. By 1907, in *The Autoerotic Aspects of Singles,* Freud went so far as to claim that tennis could even be enjoyed when the net is down.

rible apprehension prevails as the frightened masses begin to realize something they had always suspected but never dared admit: sex is not a natural activity. It cannot even be called a perversion; worse than that, it is now scientifically proven to be nothing more than a nervous habit, a compulsion at best. As Freud observed in reference to the proliferation of sex manuals even in his day, "If thick tomes have to be written in such great detail about how to perform in the bedroom, then sex is no more or less a hobby than building a bookshelf" (1911).

Entirely new strains of neuroses and psychoses are appearing in all segments of the population: the Sunday Depression (facing the weekend without a game), Acute Tennis Interruptus (the haunting fear that the bell will ring in the middle of a set), Tennis Narapoia (a deeply regressed defense against paranoia, characterized by the strong suspicion that one's opponents are making fair line calls) and the Tennis Bereavement Syndrome (a shock reaction to losing a spouse to the ravages of the Tennis Obsession).

Concurrently, the very symptoms of neurosis that face patients seeking psychiatric treatment are found in the analysts themselves. How can one sincerely interpret away a pathological Tennis Urge if he himself secretly assigns tennis a dangerous priority in his own life? Analysts almost unanimously admit to secret pangs of jealousy as they try soberly to explain to a patient that he is avoiding intimacy and acting irresponsibly toward work and family by playing in Sunday morning leagues and participating in early-bird specials (7–9:30 A.M., weekdays). Here they are, appealing to the patient's sense of justice, maturity and good conscience, while they themselves sit in stuffy offices on nice days, dreaming of themselves out on the court and watching their lives pass by. For the first time in the history of psychoanalysis, the neurosis seems far more appealing than its cure. The pleasure derived from discussing rackets and stringing (and the use of the tennis glove as a prophylactic), from poor-mouthing one's opponents and partners, and from complaining about the agita of mixed doubles is certainly more closely related to real life than any tired exchange about marital woes or sexual dysfunction.

Without question, the Tennis Obsession is upon us and is tearing at the very guts of the American way of life. Perhaps if we can free ourselves from the insanity that surrounds us, we may begin to achieve a clearer realization and acceptance of the ruthless, unrelenting nature of the Tennis Urge as one of life's givens. Let us go back in time in order to gain some historical perspective by tracing the progressive development of Der Ursprungliche (Tennis Lust) as a concept.

Was Freud Mentally Unsound?

SIGMUND FREUD was as complex and human as the rest of us. But the known circumstances of his life, filled in by the multitudinous details of a very considerable correspondence, suggest that those who see in his theories a covert personal sexuality or who endow him with a lurid clandestine tennis life are covering a sheep with wolf's clothing. The most intimate glimpses into Freud's state of mind are provided by three letters written during the turbulent years between 1901 and 1903.

July 17, 1901

Dear Dr. Jones:*

I am writing to you as an intimate of Herr Professor. Frankly speaking, I am worried about him. His tone seems so urgent and anxious these days. A strange, otherworldly expression comes over his face when he talks of tennis. Dr. Freud is usually so scrupulous and scientific in his formulations. His feelings on the subject of tennis and its vicissitudes, however, are so intense and overwhelming that at times he seems almost a convinced believer. If it weren't for his stature and the magnificence of his previous works, I would wonder about his emotional stability. I patiently accepted all of this with a wait-and-see attitude until last week, when Dr. Freud whispered to me that I should meet him "on the tennis court on Sunday morning at 7:30 and not tell anybody." I am waiting for your reply as to how I should interpret this.

M. Chasen

---

* Ernest Jones is best known today for his scholarly biography of Sigmund Freud. Earlier in his career, he developed his reputation after fleeing England to Canada in a storm of controversy about his questionable methods of treating little children. In 1928 he was expelled from Canada for his introduction to the North American continent of the game of Canadian Doubles, a bastardization of tennis played two against one. The Canadian authorities saw through this thinly disguised attempt to ensnare innocent victims in the web of the Continental disease known as "ménage à trois," and Dr. Jones was advised to control himself until the next boat out; otherwise he'd be jailed.

September 12, 1901

Dr. Pfister:*

Civilization describes the whole sum of the achievements and regulations that distinguish our lives from those of our animal ancestors. Duty, cleanliness and order occupy a special position among the requirements of civilization. No features seem better to characterize culture and refinement than esteem for and encouragement of man's higher mental activities, his

A vintage photo of Freud at midcourt, preparing for the approach shot that was said to be the strongest stroke in his repertoire (note the fierce determination and almost gloating mastery). Most authorities agree that if he had not been preoccupied with his other interests, Freud could have been a high intermediate.

* Oskar Pfister was a pastoral counselor who became an early supporter of Tennis Instinct Theory. He is perhaps best known for his inspirational book, *God Is My Doubles Partner.*

intellectual, scientific and artistic achievements, and the leading role assigned to ideas in human life. How is it, then, that my mind is in a ferment with something so elemental as this tennis madness? I cannot sleep, I have lost my appetite, I have lost interest in my work. I am obsessed by seeking a means of escape from Martha and Anna so I may romp on the courts like an ordinary man. My patients keep me busy living up to my reputation as Herr Doktor, my family keeps me constantly moving the office furniture around (they can't decide where my couch should go and where I should sit), and I have so little time for myself. Withal, I finally am getting in touch with the root of the conflict between ambition and my urethral eroticism (the wish to urinate in my parents' bedroom and tell Martha to get off my back).* It has to do with my father not letting me play Heinrich on the Pony like all the other boys.

Very truly yours,
Sigmund Freud

---

* In a posthumous paper titled *Leave It to Sigmund* (1947), Pfister commented on Freud's genius at converting embarrassing habits (e.g., bed-wetting, urethral eroticism) into socially useful concepts. Thus Freud developed the famous "common sense" test for choosing a good doubles partner sight unseen: "Go into the men's room at the club," he advised, "and pick the one with the steadiest, firmest urinary stream. It's much better than potluck."

August 7, 1903

My Dearest Pfister:

As you well know, I could not contemplate with any sort of comfort a life without work. Until recently, I took little delight in anything else. It is thus with a great deal of surprise and envy that I view my patients and many of my colleagues who seem to be able to carry on their normal activities and yet spend endless hours sweating and running around tennis courts. Their lack of guilt baffles me.

Ordinarily, if I cannot participate in worldly pleasures, I write a theory to explain why people who indulge themselves are neurotic. In this instance, however, my defenses against the Tennis Instinct are collapsing.* Having thoroughly analyzed myself, I am forced to admit that any inclination to squeeze the joy out of tennis derives from pure hatred and jealousy. As good and as kind as they are, I wish I could get away more from Martha and Anna, with their seriousness and practicality. I feel I would not look good in tennis shorts, and I am bound by a morbid superstition about crossing white lines. The carnal delights experienced by participants in this sport have evoked a response in me from deep within. I am tempted to reconcile this growing trend with my earlier theories of self-destructive and cannibalistic instincts, but such is the beauty of the sport that it defies easy neurotic solutions.

Yours, Sigmund

* Freud's entry in his personal diary for this date describes the previous night's dream in which the only thing he saw was the forbidding sign "Keep Off the Grass." He interpreted this as a tennis injunction more powerful than the Ten Commandments, more compelling than the Incest Taboo, and later drolly commented to A. Romer: "How else can we account for the unpopularity of grass courts?"

Through analysis of his own tennis reveries, Freud discovered that extensive probing invariably revealed that dreams attached themselves to significant childhood experiences. It also dawned on him that tennis was slowly beginning to supersede sex as the favorite movie in his mind. This extraordinary mental event captured his interest to the point where "concentrated attention on such important theoretical work as the functioning of sex glands in eels is no longer possible . . . ideas emerge and vanish; everything is in doubt." On July 12, 1897, Freud wrote to his good friend Fliess: "I feel I am in a cocoon. Who knows what beast will come out of it? I had all sorts of fleeting thoughts during the day, but now they've disappeared. I must wait for the next drive forward, which will bring them back." Later (September 4, 1897): "I have been through some kind of neurotic experience, with odd states of mind, not intelligible to consciousness—cloudy thoughts and veiled doubts with barely here and there a ray of light."*

Another decisive event took place on November 21, 1897. In a letter to Loretta Norelsky, the only

---

* Wilhelm Fliess was Freud's closest friend and confidant in the pioneering days (1894–1905). In 1902, Fliess published his classic *On the Causal Connection Between the Nose and the Sexual Organ,* in which he suggested that painful or irregular menstruation is due to masturbation ("In such cases, removal of the nose is the only known cure"). For a while, Freud entertained the incredible notion that the persuasive charlatan Fliess had indeed discovered an unrecognized truth. Then he realized that Fliess's mind had deteriorated and that the man was a dangerous influence. The final straw was Fliess's 1904 publication, *The Evils of Celery.*

woman member of the Wednesday Circle, Freud described what has come to be known as the Primal Tennis Dream. "I was daydreaming of a little boy standing on the sidelines of a tennis court while ghostly apparitions in white danced about. I had just recognized the child as myself, observing my parents playing tennis, when suddenly I was overcome with a terror of stepping across the line. I woke up screaming from this upsetting experience and knew instantly that I had stumbled upon a monumental discovery."

At this point, Freud took the pivotal step that would change his life forever. Radically swerving from his classical view of infantile sexuality as the mainspring of the human condition, he coined the dictum "Tennis truths lie everywhere; they are the essence of being."* Wonderfully creative ideas crowded his consciousness: the repressed incestuous conflicts involved with net play, the Oedipal issues that caused double faults, the close link between homosexual shame and weak backhands, the lingering fantasy of the empty tennis can. Trusted colleagues offered further evidence to support the great wisdom of the Tennis Unconscious. L. Katz, in his paper *Bisexuality and Mixed Doubles* (1904), conclusively demonstrated that the greatest problem with this perversion is one not

* There was one excess that Freud himself halted. In 1922 a necrophilic interest in tennis cremation swept through Austria. Deluged by hundreds of requests from tennis melancholics to have their ashes scattered on the tennis courts, the Austrian government, with Freud's support, put a clamp on this practice on the grounds that the courts were becoming lumpy, causing bad bounces.

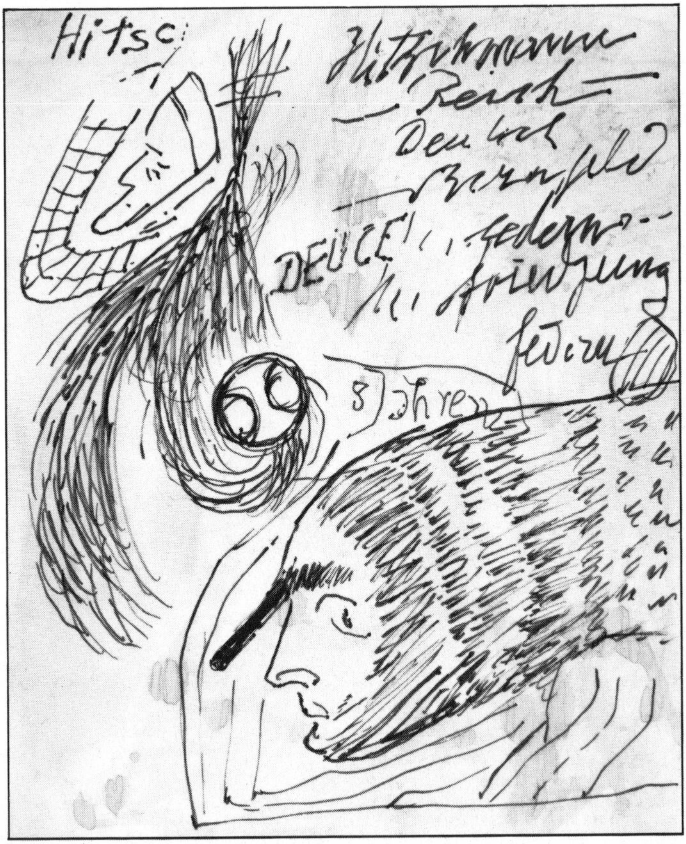

Freud's rendering of the birth of Tennis Instinct Theory. "It came to me full-blown in a dream," he recalled in Interpretation of Tennis Dreams *(1905). "I saw a man buffeted by a powerful whirlwind. Mysterious forces seemed to be rising up from inside of him. Suddenly a strange object emerged from his forehead. I could not make out what it was. Then I saw the word* Hitsc. *Over and over I repeated this unknown word to myself until finally it dawned on me: '*Hitsc *the ball!' All at once I recognized the strange object as the handle of a tennis racket. The clues were too obvious to ignore. Such was my introduction to destiny. . . ."*

of social adaptation but of deciding which team to play on. When he weighed the relative advantages of homosexuality and mixed doubles in a later revision of this powerful concept, Katz heeded Freud's sage advice ("Mixed doubles mean trouble") and finally opted for homosexuality. W. Wilner, an unorthodox, left-handed analyst, came to the startling conclusion

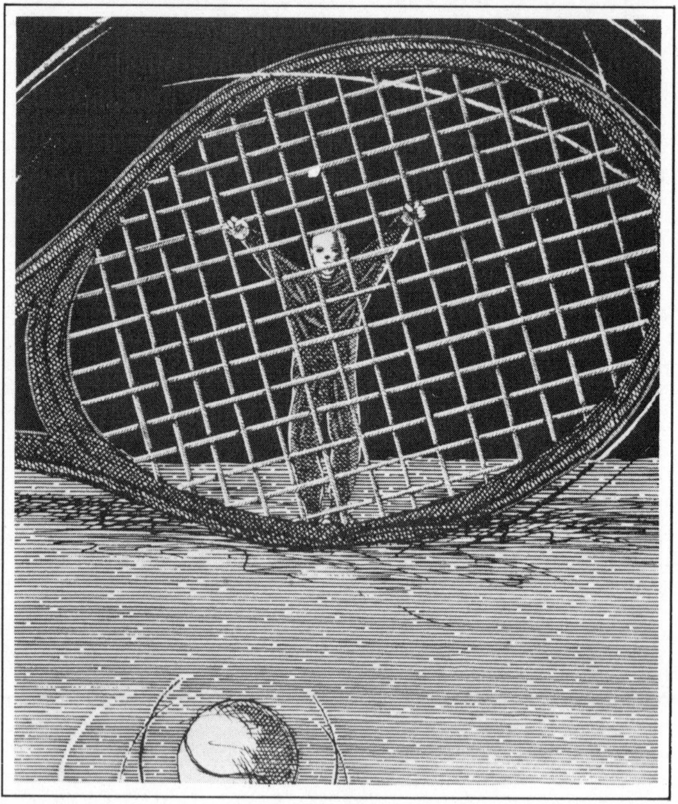

This graphic by J. Fishman was personally commissioned by Freud (1923) to depict the terrible frustrations of a child who is not yet allowed to play but is old enough to dream and wonder.

that tennis spelled backwards is "sin-net"; he shared his revelation with Freud, who was thunderstruck by this scientific confirmation of the murky, mysterious forces buried alive in the human psyche.

Nevertheless, mindful of the torrent of abuse unleashed by his relatively mild sexual hypotheses on incest, castration anxiety and the like, Freud resolved to wait till the climate was ripe for public disclosure. During the early development of Tennis Analysis, he relied increasingly on his confidants in the Wednesday Circle to provide moral support and add refinement to the eccentric byways of his tennis theories. Yet even within the inner sanctum of disciples, cross-fertilization was difficult. There were many whispers and innuendoes that Freud's secret works and his revolting Tennis Seduction Theory were grotesqueries of his imagination and symptomatic of a once fine mind gone bad. When even his staunchest supporters were appalled by the suggestion that it was traumatic and overstimulating for small children to watch their parents play tennis, Freud was moved to deny that he had really meant it.

The message Freud yearned to share with the world was that at the core of Western man's humanistic heritage lay a primitive longing for the pure, uncontaminated satisfaction symbolized by the white tennis outfit, the warm sun shining down and the soft clay beneath one's feet. (He had a different interpretation for indoor courts and Hartru surfaces.) Nostalgic, nonsensical memories of a happy, untroubled childhood were the mechanism that directed man, a creature of simple longings and basic gratifications: "All he is looking for is a place to enjoy himself and not be bothered. If his wife is kept occupied so that he can play tennis to his heart's delight without suffering guilt, this is a fine marriage! Correspondingly, if the same individual can fixate his libido on the ball without getting distracted and worried about his responsibilities to the world about him, this is the ultimate in healthy living—with full involvement in the here and now." Freud saw this interpretation of man's basic nature as the royal road to the unconscious and a secure foundation for the future of psychoanalysis. The final determination of the tennis court as the proper arena for scientific investigation of human existence (*Approaching Nirvana: Two Hours of Tennis and a Good Cigar*, 1908) was a watershed for psychoanalysis.

Freud came to abandon the awkward machinery and abstract metapsychology of psychoanalysis as he relied more and more on demonstrations of nutsy behavior on the tennis court. Thus his landmark concept of Tennis Interruptus, reflecting the culmination of a lifetime of thought, states that neurosis results from an inhibition, a damming up of energies: "If an individual has been immersed in his work, stressed by his family obligations or put upon by extensive sexual activity to the point where he is prevented from playing sufficient tennis, this is not good. The resulting tension is subcortically transformed into anxiety."

In the face of ridicule and accusations of depravity, Freud pursued his theory with single-minded purpose and indomitable courage. It was during this period that he wrote in a letter to K. Burger: "I understand why people regard me as a tennis-obsessed psychopath. Their revulsion only masks their fright. The great primal Tennis Urge and its vicissitudes have shifted the power base in the human psyche from the relatively benign sexual drives to the more primitive Tennis Lust. In this way, I fear that I have upset the delicate balance of nature by undermining the orthodox belief of Western man. I stand unfazed by the abuse heaped upon me. They may laugh at my doctrines by day, but I am sure they dream of them by night."

The strain and pressures took a terrible toll, however, and Freud's dissatisfaction with his next effort, *My Kingdom Is Clay* (1909), compelled him to devise an entirely new strategy: the diabolical Red Herring Theory of Sexuality. With the assistance of a nuclear cell of seven trusted cohorts he began to turn out his *Project for the Scientific Study of Sex,* a series of clever diversionary articles on infantile sexuality and Oedipal formulations, while in secret he fine-tuned his beloved Tennis Neurosis Theory. Out of this feverish climate came the great clandestine works *Sexual Perversions Revealed by the Two-Handed Backhand* (1910), *Penis Envy and the Prince Racket* (1912) and *Carnal Passions and the Dink Shot* (1913).*

* In this great work Freud explored the strange custom of compulsively measuring the height of the net. "Not every man believes that the penis shrinks as he gets older, nor does every woman suffer from penis envy; therefore, we cannot explain the perverse pleasure gleaned from measuring simply on a sexual basis. The unrequited wish to be a tailor is a popular career choice, true, but this does not seem to account for many of the more extreme clinical cases that we treat. With these two great instinctual drives eliminated, the only explanation is the paranoid hypothesis that the net is actually higher on your own side of the court."

THE BIRTH OF GROUP TENNIS THERAPY

A huge barn situated 125 miles southeast of Vienna, at Bad Homburg, housed the tennis facility shown above. In 1973 the Austrian government, recognizing its potential as a tourist attraction, turned it into the National Austrian Tennis Neurotic Museum (turn left at Mecklenburg, drive 7 miles down the road to Schwevian, turn right and proceed 3 miles to Heligendamin).

The Schloss Belle-Vue in-patient facility for Tennis Incurables located outside Vienna (1897). Through his early work with hopeless cases of hereditary tennis degeneracy, Freud acquainted himself with the Great Secrets of the Tennis Unconscious ("The tennis insane can be understood as having the same basic desires as other men; they just overdo it").

Sigmund Freud's Psychoanalytic Tennis Institute. By 1906, Freud had tired of working with the garden-variety Victorian hysterics who constituted the greater part of his patient population in Vienna. Together with some trusted colleagues, he opened the clandestine clinic that devoted itself exclusively to the study and treatment of Tennis Neurose (Tennis Neurosis). Pictured above is the anteroom where patients anxiously awaited their precious hour on the tennis couch.

Quite possibly, Freud's splendid isolation contributed to even greater heights of creative inspiration. In the winter of 1914, his work at the Psychoanalytic Tennis Institute at Riemerlehen confirmed one of his deepest suspicions: "The defensive lob is not only compensatory for a small penis, but possibly its cause as well."* Yet even then, and over the ensuing years, Freud, the disciplined scientist, kept his frustrations in check and shared his heretical observations only with his closest associates.** Such a prophetic observation as "Nowadays sex is hardly worth talking about" (1923) and the unforgettable, very controversial article *Fellatio and the Short Volley* (1923) were so antithetical to Freud's "sexual" reputation that he had to content himself with developing fresh concepts and seeking objective evidence until the time was ripe.

* One of Freud's greatest successes during this period involved the case of Werner von O., a man tortured by the terrible sexual symptom of invariably missing his wife and entering the pillowcase. Dipping deep into his tennis wisdom, Freud recollected that the net is at its lowest in the middle and suggested that his patient fantasize a dipped net every time he performed. "This will not only excite you," Freud told the astounded Prussian, "it will also improve your aim." Wonder of wonders, the symptom immediately disappeared—except for the fact that Von O.'s legs kept getting tangled up.

** In *Aladdin Wasn't Rubbing His Lamp*, for example, Freud shifted his emphasis from the relatively harmless correlation between the backswing and masturbation in his first draft (1897) to a more serious inquiry into a popular Victorian fetish, the perverted use of racket covers with zippers and big teeth (1922).

"The Court Is My Couch"

A GREAT TRADITION was being established. With Sigmund Freud's encouragement and direction, the original Wednesday Circle, reinforced by apprentice tennis analysts, initiated the dawn of a new age of discovery: the Tennis Instinct Era. Spurred on by Freud's unflagging energy and the stimulus of his latest work, *The Court Is My Couch* (1924), these early zealots tested and reformulated man's tennis destiny in the transparent crucible of the tennis court.*

Until this time, Freud had been naïvely monopolized by his role as a dedicated physician with "the need to cure and to help." Whatever his other beliefs, results from the couch came first. With the evolution of the Tennis Instinct, however, Freud made a fundamental switch in technique. For severely practical reasons, he had always perceived the analyst as an objective outsider listening to his patients' recollections, sifting, sorting, interpreting, but never becoming personally involved. There were, of course, the problems of transference, countertransference and yawning, but these were minor problems and could be dealt with through care, common sense and discipline.

* Freud's famous tennis case studies are pure works of art. Who will ever forget the String Man, Hanna O., the Net Man, Little Hands, the Racketeer and the Wolf Man? This extraordinary assemblage of detached clinical observations preserved for posterity the living drama of Tennis Psychoanalysis.

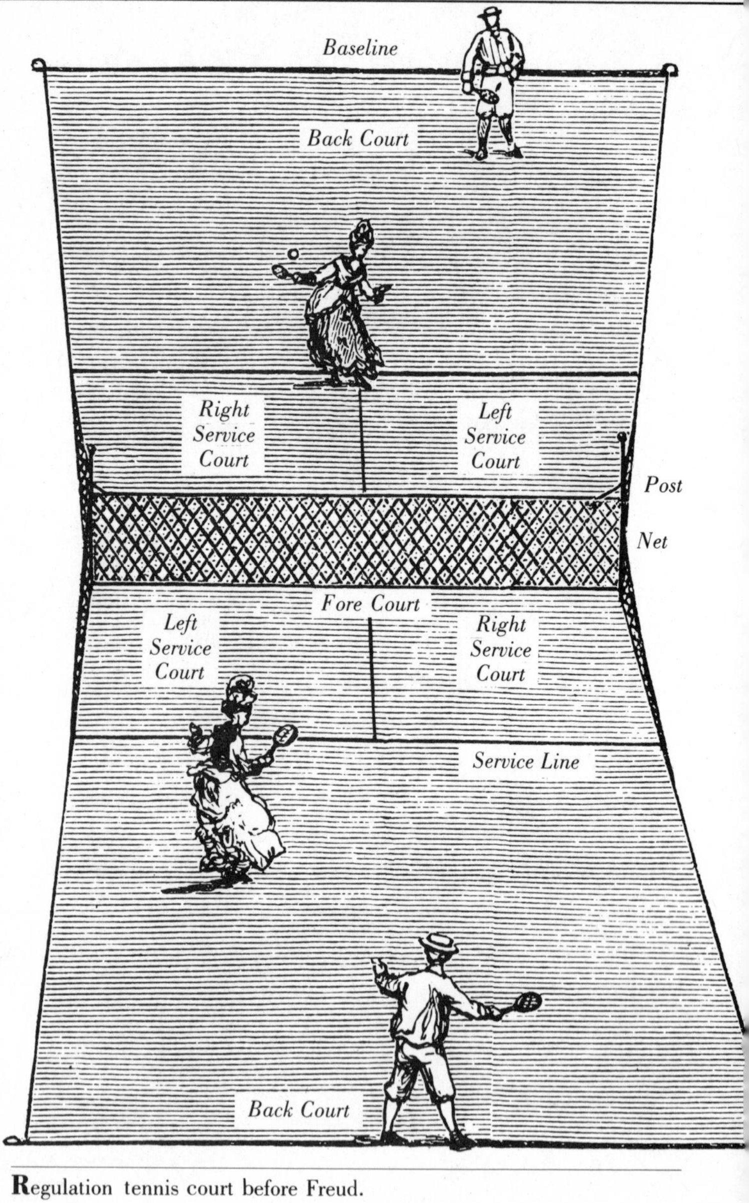

Regulation tennis court before Freud.

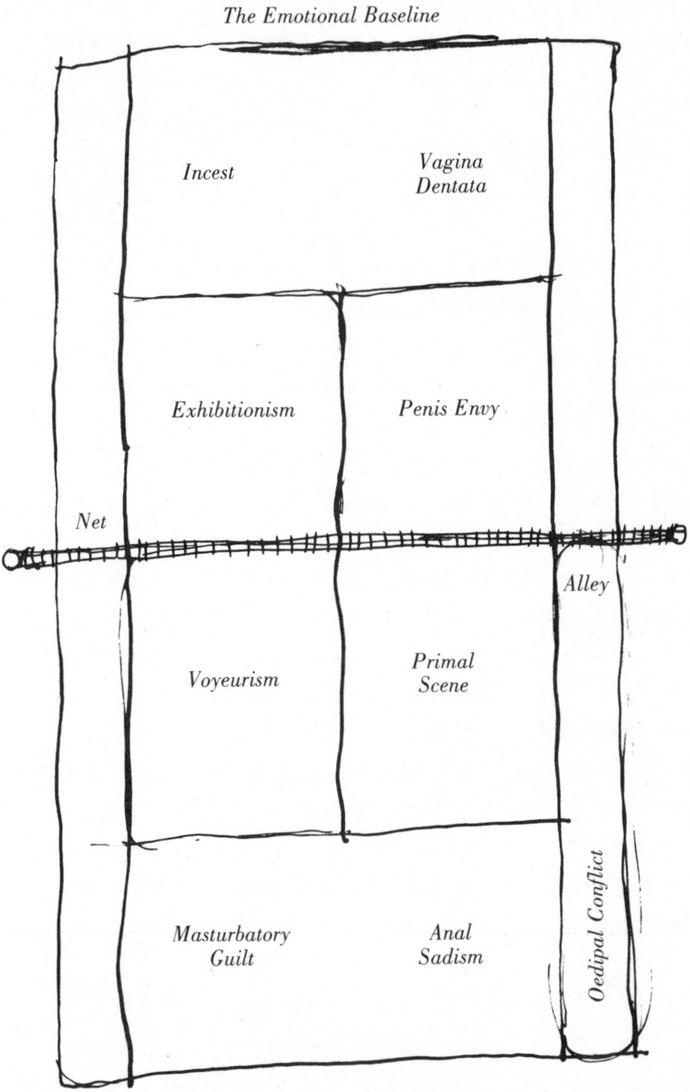

The tennis court in psychological terms, rendered by an unknown artist from Freud's personal description.

Now Freud adopted the more daring approach that lack of parental love, manifesting itself through ambivalence toward the children's overtures with regard to playing tennis, lay at the root of much mental anguish. This could be remedied and compensated for if the analyst modified his technique and assumed a more personal attitude toward his patients. Slowly, Freud's own basic tenets gave way to his burgeoning interest in the details of each patient's tennis background: the deprivations and trauma he suffered; the various rackets he used, as well as how they were strung and the pressures they were under; where he bought his equipment; the tennis outfits he wore; who he played with and what he felt when he played.* Finally Freud took the great leap forward when he stated categorically that "the only way to know one's patients is to play tennis with them."

Freud's masterly decision to enter into the real life of the patient and make naturalistic observations was by no means an impulsive move, of course, and was actually based on sound clinical evidence. Gaining impetus from the now famous dream of Otto M., where a human being was revealed to be symbolized by a tennis racket and a tennis game came to represent human existence itself, Freud intuitively realized that

* The dreaded Tennis Inquiry was a technique that often penetrated the most private and minute details of the patient's tennis life, habits and experiences. This approach was so frightening in its time that Freud once remarked, "I do not know whether such fathoming of these most intimate quirks can in all circumstances be considered legitimate, even on the part of the most high-principled physician."

"life is tennis and tennis is life." Where else but on a tennis court could one get to the deep unconscious roots of the fear of large people,* the erotic enjoyment of one's own smell and the disgusting anal compulsion to wipe the sweat off the brow with one's bare hands? The acting out of unconscious murderous infantile sibling rivalries through accidentally on purpose losing count of the score and the vile, disgusting psychosomatic basis for tennis elbow were so dismaying that Freud could barely write about them. (He once remarked to Alfred Adler that "a real gentleman does not possess such a terrible unconscious.")

It was around this time (1924) that Freud started quoting Erasmus, "The highest form of bliss is living with a certain amount of folly," and repeating "*Das ist mir ja gaz worst*" ("So who cares?") whenever his colleagues critically questioned his more radical theories. According to most psychohistorians, this stance was an indication that in the ripening wisdom of his old age Freud, the hard-nosed scientist, the gloomy cynic, had begun to mellow.

By the mid-'20s, Freud had espoused a more charitable, more whimsical and benign view of the world, for which he credited a jazz musician whom he treated in his workaday practice in Vienna. In free-tennis-associations relative to an intractable pain in his arm that interfered with lifting his trumpet to his lips, this man had said almost as an aside: "The neck-

* Margaret Mead and England's Phyllis Fitz-Hume addressed this issue in their illustrated volume *Headhunting: A Cultural Comparison of New Guinea and Wimbledon* (1973).

bone is connected to the anklebone, but who knows what's in between?" Working with these preconscious fragments, Freud gradually reconstructed aggressive and murderous impulses whose locus was displaced from above (thinking bad thoughts) and below (feeling dirty sexual feelings) to somewhere in between. Through careful research with the rest of his patients and consultation with his colleagues, he averaged out the ankle and the neck and arrived at the elbow. The great challenge that lay before him was to understand the primordial symbolic meaning buried at this site. Once he grasped that the elbow's very existence served as a screen memory masking horrible infantile and childhood tennis recollections, the nature of which was too painful and traumatic even to imagine, great vistas opened up in the treatment of most forms of mental illness.

By the 1930s fascism was on the rise, many of Freud's early disciples had deserted him or died, and his illness was growing worse. Against this unpromising canvas, Freud concluded that the world was still not ready to face reality. He continued to write prolifically, turning out a tremendous body of work for a man his age. His searing paper *Incest Is a Family Affair* (1931), co-authored with his beloved daughter Anna, is testimony to his uncompromising honesty. In this remarkable work, Freud authoritatively exposed the anal-sadistically based offensive lob as the underhanded shot that it really is: "The lob must be given its chance, but this is a disgusting stroke to use in mixed company if its sexual and exhibitionistic roots are not honestly acknowledged and properly analyzed."

Shortly thereafter Freud published *The Traumatic Roots of the Electra Complex* (1932), in which he unraveled the masochistic basis for little girls' attachment to their fathers ("It does little harm to a girl that she has no penis; the father continuously yelling at her to put out the lights is the problem").

Great work followed upon great work in an incredible display of virtuosity: *Fuzzy Balls and Pubic Hair*; *Flakiness on the Tennis Court (or, The Mental Anguish of Dandruff)*; *Enjoying Your Mishits: The Power of Negative Thinking*; *Civilized Tennis Morality and Modern Nervousness*. The seriousness with which Freud viewed these concepts is best illustrated by his sober reminder, two years before his death, that "the awesome healing power of the Tennis Unbewusstsein (Tennis Unconsciousness) is man's best answer to the death instinct" (in *The Nightmare of the Canceled Tennis Game: A Study in Obesity, Perversion and Suicide*). His final known work, *The Reach Should Not Exceed the Grasp* (1938), is so complex, so multilayered, that it remains for future generations of scholars to unearth its hidden meaning.

To these scholars, Freud's semimystical statements deriving directly from Tennis Instinct Theory offer fresh hope and certainly a more interesting response to human suffering than the tired, empty enticements of sexuality. (As Freud wisely observed about the act of intercourse, "Once you've had it, what do you have?") His hypotheses are enduring, classic contributions, seeds of the long awaited general model of human behavior. While on the surface tennis may seem to be merely another sport, Freud suggests that

Anna Freud was an avid tennis player. When Austro-Hungary ran out of tennis balls during World War I, Freud dealt with his daughter's deprivation depression by playing imaginary games with her without tennis balls. The photo above, taken during one of these matches, clearly indicates Anna's weakness for shots hit down the middle (which, symbolically speaking, may account for her remaining virginal for the longest time).

its creation was above all a means to an end: "The very structure of the game opens possibilities to human insights and understandings that previously would have been impossible" (1934). Tennis, to Freud, represented a vehicle for self-expression, a broad screen upon which life can be projected in infinite detail: "In modern times I identify tennis as a cathartic outlet that is most necessary not only for the understanding but for the survival of the species.* The putrefaction and decay of sexual interest and the problems that go with it have undoubtedly hastened the development and emergence of the Tennis Urge" (1932). For Freud, tennis was the metaphor of our time.

* Six chronically compulsive lobbers were spared the harsh option of banishment from their tennis club or involuntary lobotomy as a result of a more humane interpretation of their antisocial behavior.

... Konzeptionen dargelegt und habe mein Frühst...
...ändnis der starken Beschaffenheit dieses Mom...
...binationen von einer hervorstechenden Methode der...
...ender Ratten auf das Gesäß gebunden ...
...l hatte, entwickelte ein seltsames Tennis-
...spiel, würde er vor Furcht gelähmt. Und
entwendet, habe ich noch ...
dieser „Tennis" Szene ...
der Tennisschläger
Ratten-Verbindung
einem neuen Natur...
daß mein Patient...
wenn er den Kon...
sei so unrealistisch un...
unabänderlich zu...
mit dem Rotieren...

...ischen
...nis-
...schläger

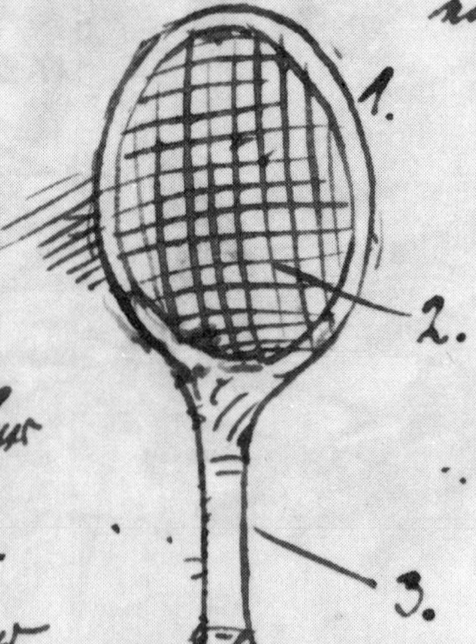

...e Absurdität dieses Zusammenhangs herauszu...
...fessionelle Hilfe gesucht. Als sich der...
...amt hatte, löste sich dieser Widerstand...
...atte der Patient auf den Tennisschl...
...e masochistische sexuelle Erregung...
...iese Form von Perversion konnte...
...e. Und um seine morbide Libido z...

AN ANNOTATED SELECTION OF SIGMUND FREUD'S SECRET WRITINGS

THE PAPERS CONTAINED in this section have been translated from the original German manuscript. It has not been an easy task to render Freud's prose, with all its depth and passion, into the English language.* Whenever his writings became difficult or obscure, it was necessary to move closer to a literal translation at the cost of stylistic elegance. Another obstacle was that Sigmund Freud tended to use certain terms interchangeably and to revise his thinking over the years with no explicit acknowledgment. For purposes of clarity, the terms Tennis Instinkt (Tennis Instinct) and Tennis Trieb (Tennis Drive) will be used synonymously. Der Grosse Tennis Drang (the Great Big Tennis Urge), however, is intended to connote something even more basic, a primeval all-consuming pleasure lust.

As a writer, Freud was opposed to a preoccupation with consistency but fiercely resented being considered willy-nilly; instead, he preferred a fragmentary treatment of a subject that encouraged further exploration rather than premature closure. This was particularly true of the early period in his work, when he became so excited about discovering the uncon-

* It is not clear, for example, whether Freud meant some of his statements literally. In outlining a case study of tennis homicide, Freud describes a man who murdered his long-time doubles partner for daring to say "Make it good" after the man had double-faulted twice before in the same set. Did Freud mean that the man wished harm or was he a real killer?

scious roots of top spin that he jumped around and hardly knew what to do with himself. One of the aims of this book is to show the continuity and modification of Freud's ideas as they developed.* This historical approach is valuable as an antidote both to uncritical acceptance and to ignorant rejection of Tennis Instinct concepts. It is beyond the scope of this single volume to attempt to fully present Tennis Instinct Theory. This section is intended more as an introduction, as a sort of stimulant to interest the reader in going back to the original sources. The major thrust is to present the real Freud—no longer burdened by abstract, scholarly connotations, but full of life and pithy remarks. Those readers who have the patience to retrace the path that Freud first followed in developing and then strategically discarding the naïve sexual libido theory, who share the problems, understand the errors Freud made, the partial truths and finally the fundamental discoveries of the Tennis Instinct Theory, are embarking on the adventure of a lifetime.

* An example of this is a paper written in 1910, *Rough or Smooth?*, which reflects Freud's inquiry into the probable childhood experiences that enabled certain individuals to win the toss for serve more frequently. The only variable that distinguished winners from losers was that the mothers of the former had bathed them to age sixteen, and by 1912 Freud realized this was an embarrassing finding. He dropped his interest in the subject with the statement, "Sometimes you can go too far."

The Oedipal Triumph: A Psychoanalytic Inquiry into Why You Lose to Worse Players

*One of Freud's most provocative papers describes the case of Little Hans, a championship tennis player who invariably lost his most important matches. In the following excerpt, Hans' infantile hysterical fear of animals is revealed as the source of his castration anxiety.**

As a young boy, Hans refused to go out in the street because he was afraid a horse would bite off the head of his tennis racket. He was in a jealous and hostile Oedipal relationship with his father, who had taught him the game but harbored unconscious competitive anxiety about being beaten by his son. Hans dearly loved the father but had repressed a hostile instinctual impulse toward him. . . . He alleged that what he was afraid of was the horse's bite. The idea of the father's retaliatory vindictiveness for his son's competitive strivings was projected onto the horse. I helped Little

* It was in an early paper, *Tennis Secrets* (1897), that Freud first introduced the powerful technique whereby patients were encouraged to unburden themselves of their most terrible tennis memories ("The whole undertaking is lost if a single concession is made to secrecy"). The torment of impacted self-recrimination was almost too terrible to listen to, but Freud's partial loss of concentration proved a godsend.

Hans, the tournament failure, to see that he could not beat his opponents because in rousing himself to dislike them enough he would injure the symbol of his beloved father.

After many months of working through this insight, Hans is now winning many tournaments and there is no residue of the childhood fear that a horse will bite into his racket. He *is* afraid that a horse will someday bite off his genitals and castrate him, but this is only a mild preoccupation; with the replacement of the horse by the automobile, such a phobia will soon be an anachronism.

—*The Unconscious Need to Fail*, 1896

The Illusory Security of the Prince Racket

A colleague has sadly informed me of the passing of the Davis Cup wooden racket. Once the most popular choice, this old standard is being phased out in favor of the Prince, the Big Bubba and other rackets with bigger and more aggressive heads. Since in fantasies, dreams and numerous symptoms the head is the symbol of the male genital, the anxious attitude that bigger is better is a fruitless, compensatory activity. Patients who suffer an abhorrence of their poor play with conventional rackets experience this as symbolic of castration anxiety and try desperately to escape into the false security of hard metal and big heads. These substitutes for penises may provide temporary flashes of success, but the neurotic inferiorities are only displaced elsewhere. Remember the popularity of the hat? Where is the hat today? When people finally came to the realization that the hat extends the head but is detachable and must be constantly tipped to one's neighbor, it fell into disrepute. I fear that it won't be too long before users of the Prince racket begin to develop complexes that their actual penises are poor, undersized replacements for the real thing. . . .

—*The Prince Racket: Symbol and Symptom,* 1899

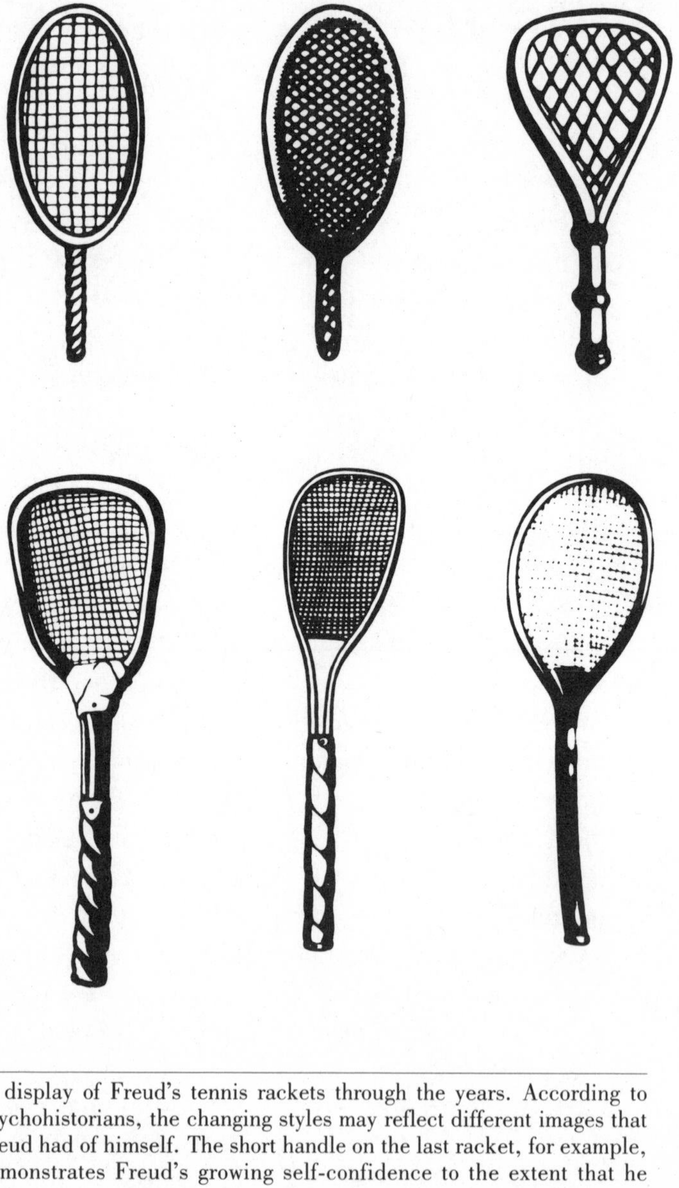

A display of Freud's tennis rackets through the years. According to psychohistorians, the changing styles may reflect different images that Freud had of himself. The short handle on the last racket, for example, demonstrates Freud's growing self-confidence to the extent that he

grandiosely began to believe his arm was as long as his penis. In truth, Freud could never really decide whether penises were symbolic of tennis rackets or tennis rackets were symbolic of penises.

THE PSYCHOPATHOLOGY OF MIXED DOUBLES

The Oedipus complex, revealed as an essential phenomenon in the sexual period of early childhood, ultimately succumbs through repression and is followed by the latency period. While an early theory of mine attributed its destruction to a lack of success, my most recent formulation is that what brings about the destruction of the child's phallic genital organization is the threat of castration.* To begin with, the boy does not believe in this threat or heed it in the least. Not until he observes the puniness of little girls' forehand and backhand strokes, as well as the labored thrusts of their service efforts, is his disbelief suspended. His unconscious fantasy tells him that these were once little boys who were punished for their dirty thoughts. The dread fear of hitting like a girl and being sent packing to sleep-away tennis camp results in desexualization and sublimation of the libidinal trends belonging to the Oedipus complex. The tennis potential is preserved through the repressive renunciation of sex and the delayed pursuit of erotic interests until marriage. Sex persists in a preconscious state during this latency period only to be reunited with the tennis urge

* Freud never fully resolved the Oedipal issue. His final word on the matter, in 1936, was that boys will renounce their incestuous urges when they discover that their mothers are sexually unappealing.

in early adulthood; the subtle melding of sex and tennis through wedlock is one of the foundations of young love. The gradual erosive effect of playing mixed doubles with one's spouse is not felt until the thirties and forties. The flagrant disregard for reality and the generally poor judgment displayed by those who choose to risk their marriage on the Scylla and Charybdis of this infernal invention reflect masochism at its worst.

—*Dissolution of the*
Oedipus Complex, 1903

Preliminary Communication on Tennis Elbow

Neurotic symptoms such as tennis elbow stem from a conflict that arises over a new method of satisfying the libido. The path to perversion branches off sharply from this to neurosis. The libido's escape under conditions of conflict is made possible by the presence of fixation . . . the libido finds the fixations required to break through the repressions in the activities and experiences of infantile sexuality. The symptoms create a substitute for the frustrated desire by means of a regression of the libido to earlier times. Among the occurrences noted again and again in the youthful history of neurotics are: observation of parental intercourse (the primal scene), seduction by an adult and threat of being castrated. The libido's retreat to fantasy, as an intermediate stage on the path to the formation of symptoms, seems to call for a special name. Jung calls it introversion. I call it "tennis elbow." If those wretched sufferers can only be persuaded to desist or even to reasonably curtail their compulsive masturbatory activity, particularly on the day of the game, the sharp pain usually associated with this ailment should relieve itself within a month.

—*Introductory Lectures on Tennis Psychoanalysis*, 1906

On Tennis Camp

May 21, 1908

Dear Dr. Jones:

Just a brief note on the latest neurotic symptom to hit Vienna: the wish to be sent away to Total Tennis Camp. The fact that so many normal-appearing, respectable adults are signing up for tennis is impressive even to my severest critics. These individuals are trying to "recapture" something that was never there; the childhood memory they are searching for never really existed. The pitiless culture in which we live creates psychological scars that cannot be alleviated by mini-week fantasy cures. There is no magic bullet. Tennis neurosis must be treated with the sensitivity, respect and hard work that any serious illness deserves. Only when we remove the symptoms can we restore the sick patient to his former state of health. The general course of treatment requires three times a week of singles and two times a week of doubles for at least three years. Any dilution of this regimen on the part of the patient should be regarded as resistance.

Yours truly,
Sigmund

P.S. I am attending a mini-week camp on July 28 with my friend Mortimer, but solely as a scientific observer. Please don't tell anybody.

EXHIBITIONISM AND BESTIALITY ON THE TENNIS COURT

The use of young boys and girls as retrievers of loose balls on the tennis courts is a disgusting remnant of civilization's prehistory—a barely discernible derivative of bestiality. The employment of the young (which is an extension of the ancient Waspish custom of pedophilia) is only one step removed from our most primitive roots. The etymological basis of the term "go fetch" has such obvious sadomasochistic and animalistic associations that it is hard to understand how this kind of obscenity is allowed to go unchecked. First

Alerted by Freud's Tennis Seduction theories, police investigate pedophilia and bestiality on the tennis courts.

animals, then children. What tradition will man think of next to debase? To the best of my knowledge, the unconscious link here is the primal scene. Shyness in retrieving one's balls from the next court is intimately related to coitus interruptus. People with a strong guilt complex about asking for what is theirs are defending against secret voyeuristic tendencies. But, if you follow my logic, the ball boy is a conduit for satisfying these needs without shame. Another recognizable trait in this type of individual is that he must preface going to the bathroom by announcing it to everyone first. This is a carryover from childhood, wherein the individual in question frequently disturbed the parents' foreplay by showing them how well he played. The exhibitionistic need expressed here is the origin of the term "tennis interruptus," which has to do with the frustrated compulsion to discharge one's underlying tensions through tennis.

—*Moral Decay in*
Our Time, 1909

SEX VS. TENNIS

Freud's ability to read Spanish allowed him to test the accuracy of the Spanish versions of his works, the reading of which usually provoked a lively conversation on the correct interpretation of his thoughts. On one occasion, however, Freud became very agitated. In a letter to Señor Luis López-Balesteros y de Torres, the Spanish translator, he stressed the distinction between tennis "lust" and tennis "drive."

. . . By emphasizing the erotic aspect of the tennis instinct, you may unwittingly be a victim of the Romance languages. Sex can never be mixed with tennis. The healthy individual must practice abstinence until he has the maturity of character to fuse these two great drives. To avoid misleading my Spanish readers, you must stress the relative priority of tennis over sex. Perhaps their shock will be muted if we include the following illustration: John L. Sullivan, the great American boxer, never had sex or shaved for three weeks prior to a big fight. A person can have only one thing on his mind at a time, or, as the distinguished Spanish poet José Ortega y Gasset, said: "A person cannot blow bubbles and have great thoughts on the same day. . . ."

—*Letter to Spanish translator*, 1909

GENDER BARRIERS

Nowhere are Freud's misogynistic biases more nakedly revealed than in his savage attacks on mixed doubles. Below is a letter he wrote in 1912 to socialist Emma Goldman upon reading her pamphlet, "Social Equality on the Tennis Court."

Dear Emma:

I heartily agree with your reference to mixed doubles as "the great melting pot" and "the starting point for all action and conduct." Women are indeed the cause of war and the end of peace, the basis of what is serious and the aim of justice, the key to all allusions and the meaning of all mysterious hints. The direct erotic approach has never permitted us access to the true essence of femininity. Perhaps spontaneous mingling and noncommitted partnerships in the fresh air will put an end to stolen glances, the hourly thoughts of the unchaste and the constantly recurring imagination of the chaste. You are quite right to indict sexual passion as an imperfect manifestation of man's relation to woman. The mixed doubles experiment undoubtedly offers mankind a fresh opportunity to understand the obscurity enveloping this strange gender called woman.

Affectionately yours,
Sigmund Freud

P.S. In all honesty, though, I still don't enjoy playing with my wife Martha.

Tennis and Holistic Health

Although many of his concepts met with repugnance and skepticism, Freud made one significant inroad through his tennis theories. Until 1913, Austrian parents generally forbade their children from masturbating because the prevailing wisdom of the day aroused fears of insanity, syphilis of the brain, loss of physical energy, etc. Once Freud's theory that a brisk morning masturbation was unique as a tennis warm-up exercise began to leak out, however, the repressive Victorian mores were lifted forever. The opportunity to be loose and relaxed before one got on the court and the clear edge that this wake-up exercise provided were too much for any fair observer to deny. Not right away, but gradually, masturbation was incorporated as part of the growing trend toward holistic health.

To see is not necessarily to believe. So many times I thought I had irrefutable evidence, and yet society was like a heartless stone wall. But now, perhaps, all the doubts and sorrows have been worth it. My faith in man's fairness may yet be restored. In my work-in-progress, "Beitrage zur Kenntniss der Bildung, Befruchtung und Theilunf des Tennis Eies," I discuss the foundation and fertilization of the Tennis Urge, emphasizing its genetic aspects and showing how it can bring peace and prosperity to this troubled world. God knows, if they can accept masturbation, maybe they can accept a tennis lesson from an old Jew.

—*Untraditional Warm-Up Exercises*, 1912

Selected Case Studies in Tennis Hysteria

"The quality that distinguishes Tennis Analysis from all other forms of treatment is that it is essentially and consciously a very personal form of therapy. No longer is the analyst's role that of a cool, objective observer in an antiseptic atmosphere of clinical neutrality. I choose involved participation in the vicissitudes of the tennis game that is life."*

—Freud, 1897

Sigmund Freud's open, direct, hands-on approach is best illustrated in his case histories. The following excerpts demonstrate how Freud's understanding of the presenting symptoms from a tennis perspective proved significantly cathartic in freeing his patients from their psychic suffering.

Case History #1: *The Face of Rage*

Frau Necillie C. suffered from an extremely violent facial neuralgia, appearing suddenly two or three times a year and lasting from five to ten days, that was diagnosed as a guilty self-punishment for wrongful acts. Frau C., being of weak character, frequently grimaced and ground her teeth when her partners made unforced errors; besides that, she had a terrible frown and wince. Because of Frau C.'s good upbringing, the facial symptoms were interpreted as conscience attacks for her inconsiderate behavior.

Case History #2: *Familial Jealousy*

During my visit to a tennis resort outside Vienna, a young employee named Marie approached me with the problem of an anxiety attack that had first appeared two years previously. It developed that Marie's uncle had fondled her and tried to make even further advances, which she turned away. He had already been incestuously involved with his daughter (her cousin), with whom he was a frequent partner at the Sweetheart Tournament. These references to incest and sexual traumas, and the resulting hysteria, were interesting but essentially irrelevant. The root of Marie's problem was that her father never played tennis with her and that she was actually jealous of her cousin. Marie agreed that this rang true because she had loved tennis since she was a little girl, but she was not in a position to recognize this as something she could really feel. When I saw the inappropriateness of tampering with her deeply repressed Tennis Oedipus, I simply suggested that she keep her distance from the uncle and find a nice young man to rally with.

Case History #3: *Dora's Dream*

If it is true that the causes of hysterical disorders are to be found in the intimacies of the patients' daily tennis experiences, and that hysterical symptoms are the expression of their most secret and repressed wishes, then the complete elucidation of a case of tennis hysteria involves the revelation of those intimacies and the betrayal of those secrets.

A typical recurring dream is described by Dora: "A house was on fire. My father was standing beside my bed and woke me up. I dressed quickly. Mother wanted to stop and save her two Prince Graphites, but Father said, 'I refuse to let myself and two children be burnt for the sake of your tennis rackets.'" This dream was related to Dora's presenting neurotic symptoms: a shortness of breath in the second set, avoidance of men on the court next to her, and a feeling of distress and revulsion whenever a ball lost its fuzz. The dream's latent content—the mother's rejection of Dora for her valuable rackets—was an unconscious basis for her hysterical tantrums every time she tried to play tennis. The suggestion here is that this carrying on only serves as a screen for an unconscious death wish toward the mother and a denied wish to inherit her rackets. . . .

Case History #4: *The Racket Cover and the Raincoat Neurosis*

I will now outline the case of a twenty-seven-year-old man whose libido had been diminished for some time; his preparations for using a condom took hours and were enough to make him feel that the whole act was something forced on him. He spoiled coitus for himself by grossly fearing infection and laying a foundation of alienation from sexual pleasures. A three-year intensive analysis revealed that this phobic individual had unwittingly been playing tennis without remembering to remove his racket cover. His game had deteriorated considerably as a result, with accompanying symptoms of apathy, dyspepsia and insomnia. Historical reconstruction showed that failure to remove the cover symbolically reflected a childhood defense against exhibitionism and early signs of the "raincoat neurosis."

REPRESENTATIVE PHOTOGRAPHS FROM FREUD'S TENNIS ANALYSIS CASELOAD, 1912

Siamese Twins Times Two

In the entire annals of psychoanalysis, this is easily Freud's most incredible achievement. On the stage of the Vienna State Theater in 1902, Freud saw a musical comedy act called "The Siamese Twins Times Two." Deeply saddened by the sordid exploitation of these tragically afflicted sisters, Freud determined to help them. In a private consultation, he explained the rudiments of his Tennis Instinct Theory and suggested that if he could perhaps stimulate the natural Tennis Urge in each of them, they might just spontaneously break up into doubles teams. Even Freud hadn't fully reckoned with the awful power of his concepts; these lovely young ladies emerged as full-blown individuals, totally capable of playing singles. Above is a testimonial picture taken for his before-and-after collection.

The celebrated case of the split personality. So awkward was Herr J.'s form that he seemed to go off in all directions at once. Freud restored Herr J. to mental health by turning his infirmity into an advan-

The Split Personality

tage: he convinced his patient to enter the 1907 Wimbledon Tournament as a doubles team. When Herr J. reached the semifinals as a singles entry, he realized he wasn't so bad after all.

The Wolf Man

The only known photo of the Wolf Man. This is the case that caused Freud to coin the term Polymorphous Perverse for a person who is so blatantly promiscuous that he would play tennis with just about anybody. The Wolf Man's display of debauchery and his crude, lecherous come-ons finally caused him to be banned from tennis in most civilized countries. This is the only patient who was so gross that Freud was embarrassed to be publicly associated with him. Only after his death did his wife Martha confess that he once muttered, "We all would have been better off if he'd been sent to the Russian front."

The Glove Man

Freud's heroic struggle to cure victims of phobias took him down many strange paths. The famed Glove Man was terrified at the prospect of playing the net. His castration anxiety was such that he protected himself with so many gloves that he could not raise his racket or see the ball. Freud blew away these defenses with his masterly interpretation, "A dog with five legs has no tail."

Celebrity Delusion

Among the greatest challenges in Freud's illustrious career was the mass hysteria aroused by the Celebrity Delusion, a serious form of mental illness that plagued Central Europe between 1922 and 1925. Perfectly normal-appearing individuals began taking on the mannerisms and appearances of well-known personages. In this instance, Freud attempted a frontal assault on deeply fixated beliefs through Intensive Group Tennis Therapy. From left to right: a man who believed he was Charlie Chaplin, another man who carried himself like Bill Tilden, a couple who strikingly resembled Fairbanks and Pickford, and two men who tried to become famous-looking but couldn't.

Wilhelm L. was a Peeping Tom whose compulsive tendencies got him into trouble with the law. In this vintage photo (1925), Freud has Wilhelm role-playing his strange habit of crawling under the net while the ball is still in play. Freud's explanation—"What was under your mother's skirt was only her bloomers"—was so convincing that thereafter Wilhelm was able to restrain himself until the point was over. This marks the only time in Wimbledon history that the Rules Committee permitted a male player to wear a skirt so as to reassure himself that "what you see is what you got."

Peeping Tom

Dread of the Service Box

Court virtuoso Nicoló Nota ruled Italian tennis from 1904 to 1911, then suddenly, at the height of his career, developed a dread of the service box. Here we see him being assisted off the court in a state of complete nervous exhaustion. Freud's investigation revealed a passionate rousal starting in the genital area and culminating in the erection of both big toes whenever Nota entered the service box. Under Deep Tennis Analysis, Nota admitted to the unconscious fantasy behind his phobia: "The box looks so big, it's going to swallow me up." Freud dealt with this directly by telling his patient, "This is not a woman, this is simply a court," but to no avail: Nota retired in 1913. Years later, Freud commented to Romer: "It was best to let him think his problems were purely sexual. Actually, he was very bad at receiving serve."

The only remaining photo of the Man Who Played With Himself. Herr T.'s masturbatory habits were entrenched at such an early age that his versatility and adeptness were absolutely astounding. In this celebrated 1910 match, at which guests were challenged to judge whether the hand was actually quicker than the eye, Herr T. beat himself, 6–3, 6–2, 6–4. Freud later commented: "This is a case of narcissism in the extreme. Herr T. never found anyone who was half as interesting as himself."

The Man Who Played with Himself

THE LOB

The lob is the Cinderella stepchild of tennis, under-utilized, unrecognized and generally disparaged. The name "lob" itself is a condensation of a sexual organ, a high trajectory tennis shot and half a cooked one-pound lobster. The crude phallic connotation of having a big lob is too much for most men to tolerate. Women who can gratify their penis envy by masturbatory substitutes tend to lob frequently. The ability to think of the lob simply as a lob reduces anxiety considerably.

—*Resistance to the Lob*,
1914

FREUD'S REPUDIATION OF CARL JUNG

. . . I think I ought to tell you that I have always been a very moral human being who can subscribe to the excellent maxim: "What is moral is self-evident." I believe that when it comes to a sense of justice and consideration for others, to the dislike of making others suffer or taking advantage of them, I can measure myself with the best people I have known. I have never done anything mean or malicious, nor have I felt any temptation to do so. The only exception is that whenever I get a setup at the net, I smash it at that bastard Jung, for obvious reasons. . . .

—*Letter to James J. Putnam,* 1914

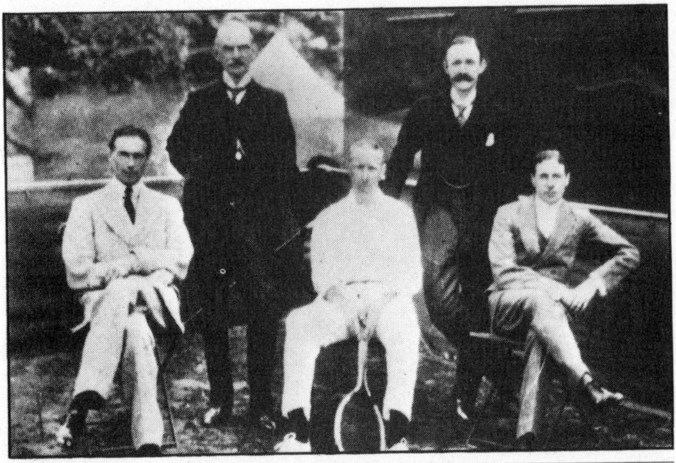

The smug Zurich contingent, led by captain Carl Jung, await their epic match with the Vienna Institute, 1911.

FREUD'S BREAK WITH ADLER

There is room enough on God's earth, and anyone who is able has a perfect right to putter about on it without being prevented. However, you poach too much on my side of the court, you distract me while I'm swinging and you mess up my game. You are one of the few people for whom I would recommend a vasectomy of the vocal cords. It is not a desirable thing for people who have ceased to understand one another, who have grown as incompatible as we have, to continue playing doubles together. Please find yourself another partner.

Yours, Sigmund

P.S. Now I know why you are best known as an expert on inferiority complexes. Go open a shoe store.

—*Freud's Declaration to Alfred Adler*, 1914

On the Transience of the Forehand and Backhand: A Study in Melancholia

The proneness to decay of all that is beautiful and perfect can give rise to two different impulses. The wistful memory of the grooved forehand and our most successful day on the courts is a precious beacon during the long, bleak season of mishits and unforced errors. Mourning over the loss of something we have loved is one of the by-products of being simply human. Yet even mourning comes to a spontaneous end. How long can somebody grieve over a lost match? When one has renounced everything and just about given up the desire to play, then the mourning has consumed itself and the libido is free to aggravate itself with fresh worries like a lousy backhand. The capacity to be preoccupied by such nonsense is one of the treasures of being alive. . . .

—*Thoughts for Our Times on a Rainy Afternoon in May*, 1916

History of an Infantile Tennis Trauma

In my seminal paper *A Child Is Being Eaten*, I analyzed how little girls develop vicarious erotic satisfaction by provoking their fathers to bite them. I went on to suggest that a common manifestation of this neurosis was losing tennis matches to opponents whom one should trounce. The concept of unconscious pleasure through pain was possibly a means of belonging. I have recently come across a similar process in several prominent male players. The one thing they had in common was belonging to wealthy Jewish families who built tennis courts on their lawns in the suburbs of Vienna. The first sign of the patients' complex was in the disturbance of their appetites. These traumatized children were exposed since early infancy, while sitting in baby carriages, to the sight of their mothers playing tennis. The deep sense of being pushed to the sidelines, unwanted and neglected, was translated in the child's mind into intense jealousy of the tennis ball. It was being hit back and forth, over and over again, but at least it was wanted. During the cannibalistic or oral phase, during which the original attachment of sexual excitation to the nutritional instinct still dominates the scene, these young ones can only ingest round yellow food substances. This is probably the best explanation science can offer for the huge popularity of matzoh balls and chicken soup.

The unconscious need to be close to the mother made the boys finicky eaters indeed. The sadistic anal organization is regarded as a continuation and development of the oral one. The anal eroticism was most noticeable in the children's morbid fascination with making perfectly round "kaka." After much probing into the unconscious, it finally occurred to me that they were vainly trying to compete with the tennis ball by trying to produce something equally appealing. The transformation of their understandable resentment into such a disgusting and masochistic project is one of the tragedies of our times. This all amply demonstrates the heinousness of prematurely exposing a male child to home tennis courts. When he graduates to maturity, the child has an unconscious need to lose so as to make himself appealing and valuable to his opponent. The poignancy of this role can be overcome only by a strong emphasis on sexual education. If he has a healthy constitution, the individual may overcome his early failure to be attractive enough to successfully compete with a tennis game by seeing his penis as a valuable appendage in its own right.

—*The Riddle of the Matzoh Ball,* 1916

TENNIS ELBOW: A PROBLEM WITHOUT A CURE

*There is strong evidence that Freud had unusual difficulty in understanding the dynamics of tennis elbow. While being distracted by writing superficial psychoanalytic articles on such insignificant issues as the distinction between repression and defense, realistic vs. neurotic anxiety, and developmental arrest vs. regression, Freud never lost sight of the challenge of the tennis elbow problem as providing a potential Rosetta Stone for an understanding of the mysteries behind all the basic neuroses.**

In conversion hysteria of the tennis elbow, the subject exhibits no anxiety whatsoever. He places a prophylactic device on his forearm, dissociates himself from the pain sensation, and patently disregards the profound physical and psychological forces converging on this sector of the anatomy. A manifold and varied picture is presented, with no uniform explanation available. The more common symptoms are motor paralysis, contractures, involuntary muscle actions or discharges,

* It was during this period that Freud wrote one of his least influential papers, *The Myth of the Sweet Spot* (1925), to point up the mindlessness of debates regarding whether the vaginal or clitoral orgasm is preferable. "Neither truly exists except in the imagination of overstimulated females," he noted. "There is no 'sweet spot' in tennis and there is no 'G spot' in women. There is only the void that is filled by fantasy."

and strange pains. These symptoms seem to fall into two groups: they are either prohibitions, precautions and expiations, or substitutive satisfactions that often appear in symbolic disguise. The elbow, falling somewhere close to the midline axis of the psychic soul, is the natural anatomical structure to express prohibitions against incest, murder, cannibalism and other pleasing obsessional states. When the individual is enjoying tennis too much, defenses against castration anxiety and other anxious accompaniments of the Oedipal complex are set into motion. Since the tennis stroke, most notably the two-handed backhand, is disturbingly similar to masturbatory movements, the titanic struggle between impulse and renunciation becomes localized in the tennis area. The truly primitive nature of these intolerable forces is evident in the masochistic satisfaction enjoyed by the tennis addict when he continues to play while suffering.* This disguised means of expiating all one's guilty thoughts and deeds through ceremonial self-punishment has provided us with the royal road to the unconscious.

—*Strange Tennis Symptoms*,
1924

*The reader is referred to Freud's masterpiece, *The Agony of Defeat and the Ecstasy of Losing* (1911), an in-depth exploration of severe masochism.

Nothing More Than a Tennis Bum

My capacity for interest is so soon exhausted. That is to say, it turns away so willingly from the present in other directions. Something in me rebels against the compulsion to go on earning money and facing my mature responsibilities. Strange secret yearnings rise in me to be nothing more than a "tennis bum."

—Letter to Sandor Ferenczi,
1922*

* Many observers have made note of the depression and pessimism that seemed to creep into Freud's correspondence starting with World War I. A variety of theoretical and personal explanations have been offered for the source of his obvious mental anguish. The most recent evidence points to the shortage of tennis balls when Austro-Hungary was at war, creating a condition that Freud referred to as Acute Tennis Deprivation. Another possibility is the "fuzz craze" that swept over the Austro-Hungarian armed forces. Hundreds of normal-appearing soldiers in the front lines, overcome by shell shock and loneliness, packed used tennis balls in their kit bags and engaged in perverted practices in the solitude of the trenches. Although his suggestion that the authorities shave the balls beforehand helped to stop the mass hysteria in its tracks, Freud never seemed to fully recover from this example of man's capacity to become nothing more than an animal during wartime.

THE UNIVERSAL MEANING OF TENNIS DREAMS

In his effort to interpret dreams, Freud recognized the stirring of evil, unmentionable, immoral, egotistical, sadistic and perverse impulses that stood in contrast to the dreamer's workaday ethical and aesthetic creed. To the mental force that keeps watch on the internal contradictions and distorts the dream's primitive instinctual impulses in favor of conventional or higher moral standards, he gave the name "tennis censorship." The universal truths revealed by the obvious tennis symbolisms of dreams were so stark in their primitive and explanatory powers that the average individual could not bear to consciously grasp their full meaning.

The depravity of the tennis grip, the naked power of the racket head, the incestuous overtones of playing on Mother Earth (clay courts) and the lewd implications of the need for a net to protect us from acting upon our erotic and aggressive drives—all are ample evidence that thinking of tennis as only a game is what keeps mankind sleeping peacefully at night."*

—*Tennis Dream Theory*, 1925

* In this incredible work Freud introduced serve-and-volley into the game of tennis and at last brought the sport into the twentieth century. Until this time, even championship players volleyed endlessly from the baseline. Freud's five-year analysis of Bill Tilden, however, revealed the destructive link between early toilet accidents and later reluctance to rush the net. The success of a player of Tilden's stature brought a slew of other high-ranking players to Freud's office.

Faulty Ground Strokes

. . . Faulty childhood interpretations of sexuality surface later on in life by interfering with one's tennis potential. False notions of fertilization through the mouth, of birth through the anus, of the vagina having teeth, of parental intercourse as something sadistic and the possession of a penis by members of both sexes constitute a formidable handicap in learning to play tennis well. Since the sexual misconceptions are often repressed and denied, the fragments of truth revealed by neurotic tennis symptomatology may be of great diagnostic and therapeutic significance. At this point, the dink shot and the lob seem the most obvious signs of gross underlying pathology.*

—*On the Sexual Theories of Children*, 1927

* In 1928 a recovered tennis psychotic, Theodor Poletsky, wrote a revealing autobiographical work, *Life Is a Bad Bounce*. In this tortured glimpse into the heart of the tennis soul, Poletsky validated the darker side of Freud's interpretation of hypochondriasis and broken strings ("Some rackets *never* get fixed") and uncovered the real cause of brown calluses.

Sexual Attraction Toward One's Tennis Racket

I know you are all interested in the case of the Rat Man. I have discussed this case at three previous congresses and until now have admitted to frustration and failure in understanding this man's strong obsessions. If you will recall, a fellow officer had described to the patient an Eastern punishment in which a pot containing live rats was strapped to a man's buttocks. Shortly after hearing this story, the patient developed an odd tennis disorder: every time he raised his arm over his head to serve, he became paralyzed with fear. Only this past year, much as a detective unravels a tangled skein of evidence, did I discover the startling meaning of his service inhibition. Realizing that rackets are strung with *catgut,* I made the rat-cat connection and returned to my patient's side with fresh impetus. It wasn't long before he tearfully confessed to me that every time he tossed the ball up and raised his arm to serve, he heard a "meow." These "meows" were so realistic and persistent that he was sure he was going insane and at one time contemplated cutting his throat with an electric razor. When he recognized the absurdity of this thought, he came to his senses and sought professional help.

Once the patient admitted to the "meow" hallucination, the guts of the case quickly revealed themselves. His anal eroticism was projected onto his tennis racket, toward which he experienced a masochistic sexual arousal each time he began to serve.* This form of perversion was too much to bear consciously; the patient repressed the morbid attraction to his racket and developed his neurotic obsession as a substitute. Once he accepted and understood his tennis racket complex, however, the animalistic fantasy died down and the hallucinatory "meows" diminished considerably. He still has trouble getting his first serve in, and occasionally he hears a "bowwow," but that seems like a small price to pay. . . .

—From Freud's keynote speech on the Rat Man, delivered to the Psychoanalytic Tennis Institute, April 22, 1928

* See the unpublished Pulitzer Prize work *Short Is Naught* (1923), a curious parable written by the eccentric genius Saul Goldberg. One of Freud's early patients, Goldberg started out writing a plea for public acceptance of stunted penis growth. The significance of the Tennis Libido slowly began to weave its way into the text, however, so that hidden between the lines is the message: "Keep the ball deep." Goldberg's playful surrealism apparently got away from him; he died penniless and unrecognized, never quite able to decide which theme to emphasize.

A Fresh Can of Balls

Each game is a fresh start, a new beginning. Generally speaking, chronic failures in real life need this re-creation. Opening up a can of three fresh new balls seems to do something momentarily uplifting for even confirmed neurotics. It holds the illusory promise of success and accomplishment.

—*Begin Each Day with a Smile*, 1929

Friday Morning and Melancholia

In this memorable paper, Freud describes a profoundly depressed individual who for seven years had played in a game on Friday mornings. Suddenly the game broke up, and the man was heartbroken. An activity he had counted on as the great love of his life, as his Rock of Gibraltar, was suddenly taken from him.

. . . He soon lost his capacity to love, ceased all interest in the outside world and every Friday morning returned to the empty tennis court to weep on the sidelines. His self-reproach reached such proportions that he began to question why his group actually disbanded. The melancholia, borrowing some of its features from mourning and others from the process of regression from narcissistic object choice to narcissism, took the obscure form that the other players had quit because he wasn't good enough for them. The nagging sense that there was actually something wrong with his play haunted and tortured him. . . .

Clearly, this case called for a drastic departure from classical techniques. Through environmental manipulation I managed to convene all the previous members of the Friday group, whereupon I asked each of them to confirm the suffering man's deepest suspicions—that he was indeed boring to play with and had no business being in the game. Their subsequent attack sparked such an outburst of self-righteous anger in the victim that he was thereafter freed from the masochistic need to denounce himself. Flushed with the sense of his own martyrdom, he promptly joined a Thursday group, soothed by the thought that he was "too nice for those other guys anyway." The masochistic libidinous attachment to the Friday group was ended forever.

—*Papers on Tennis Metapsychology*,
1930

Do-Overs

. . . We now turn to an examination of the "do-over." Players who tend to seek refuge in the judicial role have childhood histories of serving as the family referee, arbitrating differences, harmonizing and conciliating. Their great skill as moderators invested them with the need to be inoffensive and uncontroversial. The personality profiles of these players are quite different from those of individuals who enjoy taunting their opponents with catcalls of "Chinkee shows" (after an ancient Oriental philosopher known as the Chinese Solomon). This obscure Chinese slogan refers to the fact that the "true" winner of a point done over will frequently win again due to superego operations. Capricious use of "Chinkee shows" shows a viciousness of character and an ungentlemanly nature. Calculated cheating, false compliments and other forms of guerilla warfare may be the only means of neutralizing opponents who get sadistic gratification from rubbing it in.

—*The Ambivalent Character*, 1931

Existential Tennis

. . . A man is sick the moment he inquires into life's meaning and value, since objectively neither exists: by asking such questions, one is merely admitting to a store of unsatisfied libido to which something else must have happened, a kind of fermentation leading to sadness and depression. I am afraid these explanations of mine are not very profound; perhaps I am pessimistic because it's mid-September, the leaves are falling and the outdoor nets go down in two weeks.

—Letter to Leopold
Konigstein, 1931

Toe Taboos

With regard to foot faults, the unconscious conflict revolves around the forbidden lascivious fantasy of entering a woman feet first.

—*The Foot Fault*,
1932

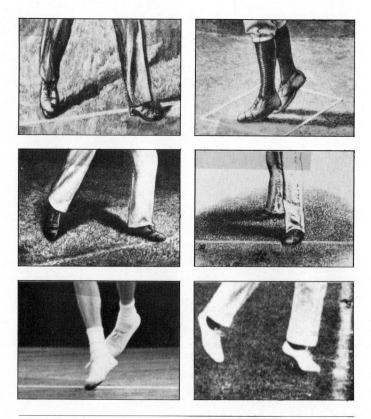

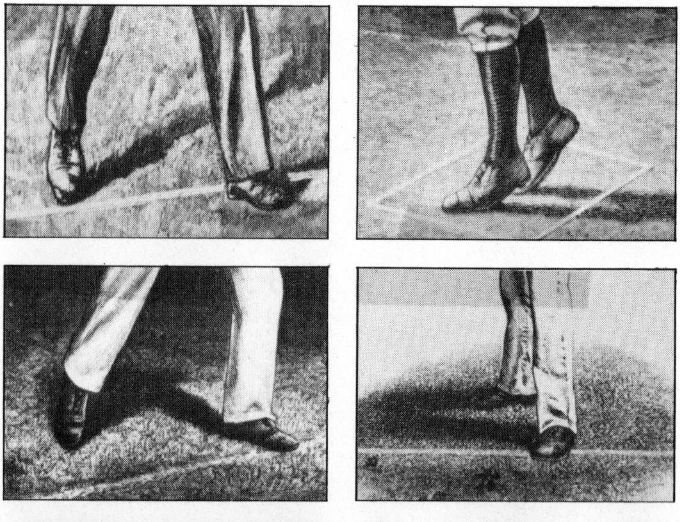

Poor Sportsmanship

The negative ego-ideal manifests itself in the form of poor sportsmanship and untoward behavior on the court.* If the ego-ideal represents the standards and values we strive for, the negative ego-ideal reflects a regression toward a repulsive image of one's self. Individuals who repeatedly engage in conduct of this kind usually have a history of enuresis, temper tantrums and petty thievery. The gross inability to be content within themselves causes them to provoke the world into being as miserable as they are. These are perfectly vile creatures who do not even deserve a psychiatric diagnosis or a club membership.

—*The McHenry Syndrome,*
1933

* Martin Hichtsky, a wild Hungarian analyst, is generally credited with being the driving force behind Freud's interest in the game. His evocative, visionary, three-volume classic, *Talk Nice to Your Racket* (1933), is considered a milestone in humanizing such a competitive sport. Unfortunately, in 1935, Hichtsky suffered a nervous breakdown, and his final two works, *The Ping and I* (a musical that closed in Budapest in one night) and *Kill the Croatians* (a murder mystery having to do with very aggressive net play), reflect the ravings of a madman. Nevertheless, Hichtsky gave Freud a lesson he never forgot: "Don't talk German to your sweet spot."

Choking Up

Most authoritative dictionaries of the German language discuss at some length the subtle connotations, denotations and implications of the word *Unheimlich* (as in Tennis Choking). To clear up this confusion, *Unheimlich* is a difficult term to define and is variously related to something frightening that suddenly takes over—the impulse to play terribly for no good reason whatsoever. I suggest a direct approach, the Heimlich maneuver, a technique designed to shock the despondent player into not being such a quitter.

—*Origin of the Tennis Heimlich Maneuver*, 1934

TROPHIES

. . . Trophy collecting indulges the hoarding instinct. The accumulation of ego accoutrements is clearly a compensation for premature ejaculation in men and for unsatisfactory orgasms or short penises in women. If these outwardly successful, socially popular individuals openly exhibit their trophies, there is strong reason to suspect an unhappy sex life. Women use male partners in mixed doubles, and often their tennis rackets, as phallic extensions of themselves. Exhibition of the trophies hides a secret shame.

—*The Secret Self*, 1934

The Freud Cup, awarded annually to the patient who underwent the most radical transformation as a result of Tennis Therapy. Eva von R. won the cup for five consecutive years, 1903–1907, but she was finally disqualified in 1908 on the grounds that she was already cured and remained in treatment solely to win the prize. A huge international debate ensued over whether anyone who was truly healthy would go to such absurd lengths to win a prize. Freud solved the problem by terminating the award and instead distributing I ♥ FREUD *buttons to those he most admired.*

THE ORIGIN OF ORGAN INFIRMITY IN WOMEN

In this excerpt, Freud presents the associations of a young girl who states that if her sister marries, she'll have a baby. The child knows that when anyone gets married, a baby comes. She says she knows a lot besides: that trees grow in the ground, for instance, and that God made the world.

What the girl was really trying to express was not the puerile, obvious thought that babies grow inside their mothers. Of course they do. In her remarks, this little girl is revealing the sexist influence of the culture on young women even at this early age. The tennis pleasure libido that is displaced by being thwarted from having one's own tennis racket and private lessons like one's big brother is transformed into erotic libido, giving rise to precocious fantasies about giving birth and so on. The abandonment of the original uninhibited love of tennis is sublimated and sexualized until it is no longer recognizable. This gross caricaturing and alteration of the deepest yearnings of little girls (to be just like their brothers) is the future source of narcissistic humiliation and inferiority. If the tennis urge was not blocked so harshly and appropriate channels were provided for the stored-up energy, women would be less filled with jealousy and paranoia about man's capacity to urinate standing up. . . .

—*Associations of a Four-Year-Old Child,* 1934

Martha Freud

Freud's review of the anthropological evidence on incest showed it to be a stronger taboo among primitive people than among the more civilized. He used the incest taboo to account for his stern admonition: "Never play tennis with your wife. It is questionable whether people in the same family should even have sex with each other, and tennis is no different."

The Road to Mental Health

Analytic treatment should be carried through, as far as possible, under privation and in a state of abstinence: no sex, in certain circumstances no tennis and no *rachmanis.** It is frustration that made the patient ill, and his dreadful tennis-related symptoms serve him as substitutive satisfactions. He must fight fire with fire. When the torn mind, divided by the epic battle between sex and tennis, temporarily renounces both these great instincts, you have the beginning of repair and ultimate cure. The great unity that forms the ego discovers an inner strength, rids itself of its sapping, unnecessary erotic aspects and faces life from a properly restored tennis perspective.

—*From an Address by Freud to His Cousins' Club Meeting*, 1935

* Yiddish for "mercy."

The Sexual Life of Human Beings

The first area of sexual interest in an infant is the mouth. The next erotogenic zone is the anus. A sign of maturity is the passing of sexual interest to the genitals. The final stage of libidinal satisfaction occurs around age forty, when man successfully subdues his superficial secondary sexual activity and turns the major thrust of his interest toward tennis. In some unusual circumstances, men in their fifties and sixties have been known to maintain some sexual appetite, but for the most part, by the late forties, the primacy of tennis is firmly established and erotic desires are now culminated through the ecstasy of the stroke.

—*The Transition from Sexuality*, 1935

The Tennis Spell

Play loses its pleasurable meaning at the point where the individual is unable to stop when he wants to. He then becomes a tennis addict. The regressive decay from relaxed play to compulsive play can be detected only by the sophisticated observer. The presence of any three of the following signs is indicative of a serious condition with poor prognosis: attending tennis camp for more than one session per summer, carrying more than one racket at a time, taking lessons and playing tennis at uncivilized hours (before 9 A.M.). Being under the "tennis spell" itself is not neurotic; the Urge is present in most adult males.

A case in point is the individual known only as the String Man. This person was so high-strung that he simply could not get tennis out of his system. Neither compulsive masturbation nor three hours of tennis daily could quench his thirst. At night, he would make obscene phone calls during which he whispered to his victim with lewd innuendo, "How do you like your rackets strung?" This repulsive habit brought the String Man to the attention of the local authorities, who contacted me. After several sessions with this individual, I was able to relieve his powerful neurotic urges by getting him a job in a pro shop where he could string women's rackets and keep his fantasies to himself.

—*Compulsive Tennis Habits*, 1935

Tennis Form

The libido bound up in competitive sports is a blending of aggressive and autoerotic drives. The functional pleasure gained is a body mastery that compensates for inferiorities and deficiencies originally experienced in childhood. This may be particularly manifested in men and women who are concerned less with winning than with looking good on the court. Symptoms include designer tennis outfits, $500 rackets, colored sneaker laces and needlepoint racket covers. The stress on form and appearance is typically suggestive of bad acne or extreme cases of shyness in adolescence.

—*The Body as a Narcissistic Instrument*, 1935

THE BALL

What is a ball? On the deepest level, it is mother or breast. Hitting a ball and having it returned is a means of overcoming abandonment fears. Unconscious association of the ball with anxiety regarding the mother's comings and goings is readily apparent in the panic that sets in when a ball is momentarily lost. Many players cannot continue the game, but must halt the action as though life itself is at stake unless the lost ball is recovered. The fact that some balls simply disappear, never to be found, is symbolic of something but I am not, as yet, sure of what.

—*The Symbolic Search for the Lost Breast of Childhood*, 1935

Killer Instinct

In the game of tennis a player calls shots in or out and, according to the rules and etiquette of the game, may have absolute jurisdiction. Since personal integrity is involved, most players reconcile this with their underlying competitive cutthroat instincts by becoming unconscious liars. Concrete evidence for this distortion of reality is hard to come by; however, present in the history of most individuals who make bad calls is the widely known nursery rhyme "When in Doubt, Call It Out."

The ruthless, predatory aspect of tennis is revealed in archaeological studies showing that the earliest ball games were played with human skulls. In French slang, each of three words for ball (*boule*, *bille* and *balle*) means "human head." The more resilient manufactured balls employed today are civilization's way of taming and harnessing our primitive, cannibalistic instincts. We actually want to murder our opponents, but we deal with this by erecting defenses that create the appearance of decency and decorum. The fundamental truths of hate and evil that must always be guarded against are immediately recognizable by any objective observer who has spent time on public tennis courts.

—*The Dark Side of the Human Psyche*, 1935

Inspired by the realization that Little Hands developed his phobias not from fear of fish but from small fingers, Freud formulated the Little Hands Test. Banned as obscene in the United States until 1935, this test involved answering such difficult questions as "Which popular childhood perversion do these grips remind you of?" and "Have you ever secretly experimented with any lewd tennis grips?" The reader will note how the grips in these photos, taken from Freud's caseload, reflect a variety of disturbances.

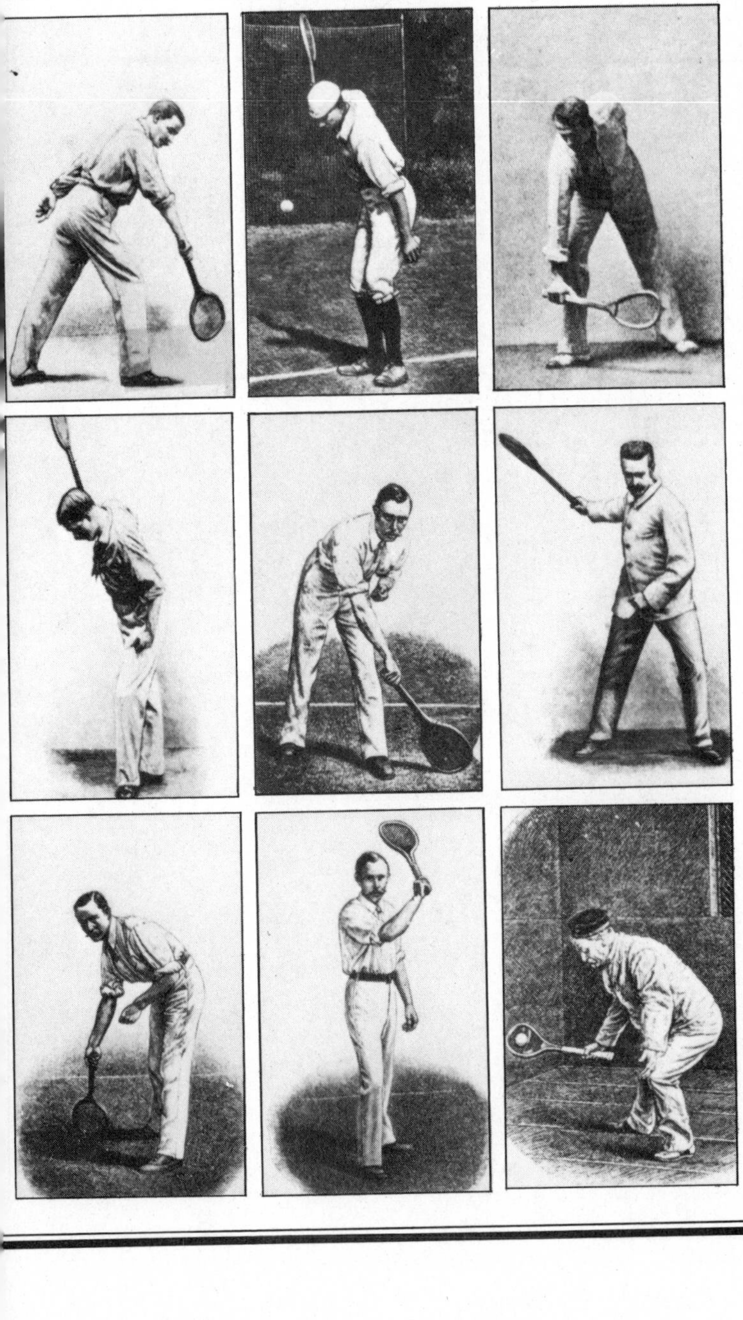

Anatomy Is Destiny

Tennis rackets have been referred to by more than one person (about eleven) as "the great equalizer." Use of oversize rackets most definitely points to problems in the sexual area. In particular, women who buy hard, metal, king-size rackets are phallic-aggressive in nature and usually were jealous of their brothers' urinary stream. These conflicted individuals strenuously attempt to compensate for their defective anatomy (penis envy) by urinating in a stand-up position, buying jeans with flies or marrying small husbands. On the tennis court they are the players who yell "First one in" instead of sticking to the rules.

—*The Unconscious Code*,
1935

The Chronic Loser

Losing badly is a derivative of encrogenesis, or soiling oneself. The shame and humiliation of defeat may have a hidden masochistic aspect. Anally fixated individuals, namely, those who were disobedient and didn't do their doody, are likely to have harsh, punitive superegos and to be highly resourceful in creating fresh opportunities to appease their unconscious guilt. If successfully treated, their blocked self-inflicted energies are liberated and their game improves rapidly. This growth spurt plus one other diagnostic criterion differentiates the player who loses due to psychogenic causes from the clearly untalented player who is constitutionally unsuited to participate in competitive games. The additional factor is the high correlation between the individual who had accidental bowel movements far into childhood and the number of unforced errors he makes as an adult. The untalented player is living up to his true potential and feels very little shame or remorse. The neurotic, anally fixated individual blames his poor performance on external conditions. This is plainly a carryover of childhood conflicts where the burden of guilt is avoided at all costs. These disturbed individuals play doubles so they can project blame on their partners, or they marry schlemiels on whom they blame all their troubles.

—*Tennis Shame and the Anal Character*, 1936

Tennis Psychology

The cunning competitor plays on the other party's guilt. Continuously praise your opponent's shots, and you'll notice how he begins to press. Self-beratement also serves to balance a guilty conscience for being successful and makes your opponent disturbed for upsetting you so. If on occasion you call one of your opponent's "out" shots "in," then later on you can innocently call an "in" shot "out" on a crucial play. Practice saying "Good try," sincerely; then you can call a lot of close shots "out" and get away with it.

—*Psychological Warfare Between the White Lines,* 1936

LOSING SERVICE

Competition between fathers and sons and between mothers and daughters often becomes intense about the time of puberty, when the physical skill of the younger player begins to match the parent's experience. Since, in the unconscious, victory is equated with murder of the father, the biblical talion principle is expected (an eye for an eye). Erratic play or losing one's nerve is best explained by the complete inability to perform if guilt is too great or the destructive urge too strong. The transition from adolescence to adulthood is immeasurably facilitated by fathers who do not have an excessive need to remain in power or who are lousy players.

—*Patricide and Self-Inflicted Defeats*, 1937

Ball Machines

Individuals who derive a warped satisfaction from hitting against ball machines feel most comfortable in sterile, inanimate environments. Prominent in their backgrounds are regularity, constancy and blandness of emotion, which led to anal-aggressive rebelliousness. These manifestly fastidious players tend to suffer from chronic constipation and harbor fantasies of being dirty in their personal hygiene.

—*Loving an Inanimate Object*, 1937

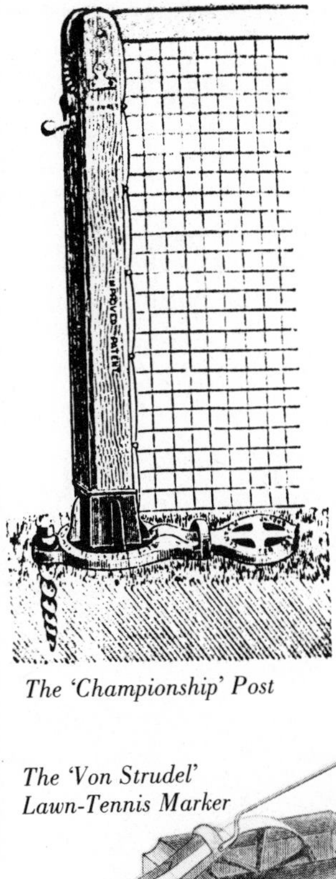

The 'Championship' Post

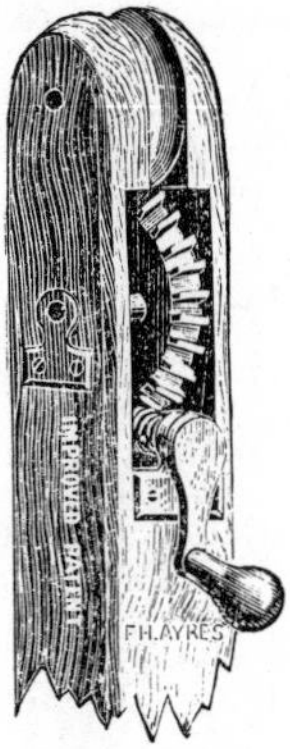

Improved Ratchet of 'Krupps' Post

The 'Von Strudel' Lawn-Tennis Marker

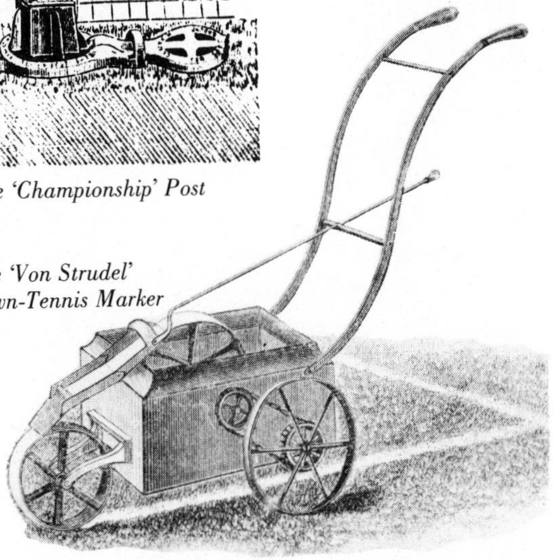

In man's long quest for what he does not know, few sagas can compare with the heroic story behind the invention and technological development of the winch, the tennis post and the chalk marker. Three of the candidate analysts at the Institute won the Nobel Prize for Science, in 1906, 1907 and 1910, for these revolutionary achievements.

Homosexuality and the White Tennis Outfit

The theory of repressed tennis instincts is probably the cornerstone for understanding neuroses. Investigation of their precipitating and underlying causes led man to search for conflicts between the subject's sexual impulses and his resistances to sexuality. I find myself searching further and further back into my patients' lives for explanations and ending by reaching the first years of their childhood, where I discovered that the seduction scenes they reported so regularly as having happened in childhood were no more than wishful fantasies. The child actually desired to be invited to play tennis with adults, to be indulged in praise as the little protegé, but this wish to be special unconsciously clashed with the effeminate association of wearing white. I would suggest that in the future tennis players wear multicolored outfits to relax these superego prohibitions, since the color white has, since time immemorial, connoted a homosexual invitation.

Returning to the seduction fantasies, these project unconscious passive-dependent tendencies. The variety of tennis grips that have been devised significantly correlate with the individual's need to be taken care of. The child's earliest grip is on the mother's breast. Difficulties in weaning have to do with doubt and uncertainty that the next developmental phase has more to offer than the former. If one cannot depend solely on Mother, then what must be learned next is the one- and two-handed masturbatory grip. Moving on to adulthood, we frequently hear the expression "Get a grip on yourself." This injunction to take command of one's life is in sharp contrast to the sloppy, passive tendency to let things slide and resist assuming responsibility for one's fate. The shifting back and forth of tennis grips is all in vain and merely symptomatic. The underlying issue is fixation at an earlier level that causes a reluctance to grow up. The secret in life is neatly embodied in the tennis stroke. Just find a natural rhythm. The wish to return to the womb denies the hidden resources in each of us.

—*The Wish to Regress*,
1937

Common Court Smells

With man's assumption of an erect posture and with the depreciation of his sense of smell, not only his anal eroticism but the whole of his sexuality threatens to fall victim to repression. This detachment from man's animal heritage is only thinly disguised lust. The position of the armpits in juxtaposition to the face, particularly during the serve, provides a secret sensual pleasure, a rush of excitation. Coupled with the inhaled accumulations derived from headbands and wristbands, olfactory eroticism has proved an important aphrodisiac for those suffering from ennui, *Weltsmerch* and overall blechiness. The preorgasmic reverie state established by this means of stimulation is expressive of an all-embracing oceanic feeling, of an intimate bond between ego and the world about us, of the sense that we are all brothers and sisters under the skin. Sweaty eroticism is therefore a modified form of sexuality in that it binds us together by a sudden acknowledgment of the genuine affection we feel toward each other. . . .

—*Man's Prehistoric Nature*, 1937

TENNIS SLIPS

Forgetting the score is intentional in nearly every case. Changing the score in one's favor frequently reflects an overriding ambition and an overdetermined need to be the winner. Strong sibling rivalries in early childhood that were never worked through and the seepage of repressed homicidal impulses reveal themselves here. On the other hand, the player who constantly gives his opponent a higher score than he deserves bears the guilt of being the favored one in our families of origin. Such an individual feels that he got more than he deserved and unconsciously finds every opportunity to expiate the guilt of his greediness. If he continuously misplaces his tennis racket, it means he is not reflective, introspective or mature enough to deal with these weighty issues and would rather spend his time sipping iced tea. Do not be deceived! Avoidance is no excuse for the wish to slip. Somewhere the unconscious will find a passage for expression.

—*Competitive Parapraxes*, 1937

LIBIDINAL TENNIS TYPES

As the libido is predominantly allocated to the province of the mental apparatus, we can distinguish three main libidinal tennis types: erotic, narcissistic and obsessional.

Erotics are those who experience multiple orgasms while engaging in tennis contests. Their passion for the game is such that they frequently reach climaxes as they are parking their cars in anticipation of a good match. When people of the erotic type fall ill because a game is canceled, they are not good enough to be included in a foursome or the weather is inclement, they are subject to severe depressions and are inconsolable.

In the narcissistic type, there is little tension between the ego and superego and there is no preponderance of erotic needs. The subject's main interest is directed to himself. He lives in a glorious cocoon populated by fantasies of how well he played, how smooth his strokes are, and how attractive and appealing he looks today. The female narcissist is so revolting in this respect that she is practically indescribable. The self-love emerging in such a case leads to a princess-like syndrome whereby the subject becomes progressively less related to those around her and substitutes adornments and fashionable outfitting for healthy enjoyment of the sport itself.

The obsessional player is the most common. He

continuously frets about his game, changes his racket and stringing often, rarely feels that he played up to his potential and tends to assume the guilt of letting his partner down. The fact is that unconsciously he loves all this worrying because it is difficult for him to care that much about any person, interest or activity. The explicit manifestations of aggravation and frustration are merely highly disguised and sublimated forms of the wanton expression of tennis eroticism.

—*Diagnosing Character Types Through Tennis*, 1937

Popular Tennis Obsessions

For several years, Freud had struggled to account for certain heretofore inexplicable phenomena of everyday life. Some individuals cannot serve, for example, unless they have all three balls in their possession. Others are preoccupied with who last supplied the balls. Still others are continuously distracted by whether or not their fly is closed. Some players cannot enjoy a sound night's sleep unless they own many different types of rackets and are fully aware of where they are at all times. Having previously traced these peculiar habits to the anatomical distinction between the sexes, Freud now made the startling discovery that in every instance the meaning and purpose of the obsession turn out, in analysis, to be the same.

The obsession is a substitute for the penis, just as the penis is the symbol for one's first racket—the earliest racket of childhood that is now gone forever. This preoccupation substitutes for the mother's penis that the child once believed in and does not want to admit no longer exists. The obsession achieves a token of triumph over the threat of castration and serves as a protection against it. Seeing that one's zipper is closed provides a measure of reassurance that everything is in its rightful place and all's well with the world. The obsessional is extremely threatened by women. He saves himself from becoming homosexual by endowing women with the characteristic that makes them powerful as sex objects. His unconscious fantasy that women really do possess a penis is fulfilled by being involved in relationships with strong, aggressive, controlling women with good first serves. A sure tip-off to these individuals is their recurring fantasy that women have an inexhaustible supply of balls under their tennis skirts. . . .

—*The Mystery Under the Skirt*, 1938

SEXUAL ENLIGHTENMENT: THE PROPER UPBRINGING OF YOUNG GIRLS

In the phallic phases of female sexual development, the clitoris is the primary erotogenic zone. With the passage of years, the clitoris should wholly or in part hand over its sensitivity and at the same time its importance to the vagina. Parents can be instrumental

Freud never fully resolved the issue of Infantile Tennis Urges. "A razor's edge exists between overstimulation and traumatic deprivation," he wrote in 1934. "Only the net divides wisdom from folly."

in helping a young girl to stop playing with herself by presenting her with a tennis racket at an early age and teaching her the two-handed grip.* Remember, idle fingers are the devil's work. Possessing the tennis racket as a substitute penis will soften the inevitable trauma stemming from a girl's realization that, unlike her brother, she has been castrated. At this stage, the latency-age girl renounces her identification with the mother as an inferior being, abandons clitoral masturbation by substituting tennis and transfers her wish to have a penis baby onto the father. The smooth transition of this phase is subject to many hazards (e.g., homosexuality, acting out of Oedipal wishes and castration fears) without the fortunate distraction and sublimation provided by the tennis interest.

—*Female Sexual Development*, 1938

* In the article "Disguised Tennis Perversions" (1909) Freud had argued that teaching little children to shake hands with their rackets is not such a good idea ("I believe in the education of the young, but to expose them to the tennis underworld at this age is corrupting and irresponsible").

Breasts, Jockstraps and the Short Volley

For big-breasted women, the forehand is easier than the backhand. It is particularly hard to follow through when one has those mountains to overcome. On the other hand, a tight jockstrap is man's punishment for not bending the knees properly on shots that are close to the net. . . .

—*Consequences of the Anatomical Distinctions Between the Sexes*, 1938

ON AN AGING BACKHAND

. . . As for me, I am no longer able to play singles with sufficient ardor. A crust of indifference is slowly creeping up on me, a fact I state without complaining. It must be connected with a decisive turn in the conflict between the two instincts (life vs. death) postulated by me, or it could be that I simply have trouble now with deep shots to the corner. . . .

—Letter to Lou Andreas Salomé,
1938

Indoor Tennis

Architectural advances that have enabled players to engage in sports during the winter months have been accompanied by some interesting symbolic designs. The bubble, for example, attracts tennis players who are generally oral-dependent with a significant resistance to growing up. These individuals romp together in a great big embryonic sac while others around them are gainfully occupied. Mostly women, they cavort in their designer outfits, make juvenile noises and generally act like a bunch of adolescents. One feels uneasy thinking that these are adults who carry little black books in which they list their weekly tennis dates that take priority over their rightful duties to their children and mates. Cooking and cleaning have become secondary to tennis lessons. I fear for the fate of modern man.

—*The Fate of Modern Man*,
1938

CONCLUSION

I HOPE THE READER of this book is suitably impressed with Freud's enduring contributions to the modernization of sexual theory. His great thesis that tennis is a natural urge whose repression has cost society dearly is driven home in many of his works with unforgettable intensity. Though his writings are often comfortably discursive and rambling in nature, Freud's passionate interest in uncovering the inner life of the Tennis Unconscious makes them most enjoyable reading. It is still a positively exhilarating experience to trace the development of Freud's early thinking (*The Net Is High*), through his middle years (*Adventures in No-Man's Land*), on up to his later writings (*The Mysterious Fate of the Underhanded Serve*).

Fortunately, Freud's extraordinarily prescient critique of modern civilization's neurotic restraints unburdens us by providing a promising solution. "We must control our environment by directing its evolution, by choosing when and how technology should be used," he wrote in 1938. "Tennis rackets and people exist not in two different worlds, but at two ends of the same continuum. Just as man has discovered that he is part of the natural world and not just surrounded by it, so also will we find ourselves intimately related to our tennis rackets. They are us and we are them. When we are able truly to accept this basic fact, we shall discover that the vain struggle to control the world about us is actually a struggle to control ourselves."

n Konzepten dargelegt und habe mein Frag
ündnis der starken Beschaffenheit dieses Mon
tinaten von einer gewöhnlichen Methode der
ander Ratten auf dem Gesäß gebunden w
t hatte, entwickelte ein seltsames Tennis
chek, wurde er von Furcht gelähmt. Und

entwickelt, habe ich erst
dieser „Tennis-Schl
der Tennisschläger
Ratten-Verbindung
einem neuen Natur
daß mein Patient
wenn er den Kon
sei so unvollständig u
widerspiegelnd zu
mit dem Rohineres

eitscher
nis-
läger

in Absurdität dieses Gedankens beunruhi
fessionelle Hilfe gesucht. Als sich der
ent hatte, löste sich dieser
atte der Patient auf den Tennisschl
n masochistische sexuelle Zwangs
iese Form von Perversion Konnt
n. Und um seine morbide Libido z
ückelte er als Ersatz diese neuart

APPENDICES

WHEN THE INFORMATION leaked out that I was assembling a book on Freud's secret Tennis Theory, several next-of-kin of the original Wednesday Circle contacted me privately. In the interest of science I was generously allowed to examine diaries and various unpublished correspondences. Those I wish to thank for permission to use this previously inaccessible material include: J. Herman, M. Romer, E. Shapiro, R. Mendelsohn, L. Bleuler, H. Deutsch, Sally Kovalchick and Lynn Strong. Personal reminiscences of Sigmund Freud, some of which are recorded below, throw fresh light on the human side of these chronicles.

I: Anecdotal Materials

MIXED DOUBLES. In actuality, Freud loved women and greatly admired them. He found mixed doubles so boring and tiresome, however, that it is said he invented the entire theory of "penis envy" to provide himself with an excuse for keeping his distance. "Women ought to be judged with tolerance and forbearance, but that's no reason for having to play with them," he confided to Alfred Adler. "They have little capacity for sublimating their instincts, they squeal too much, and besides that they don't know how to stay on their side of the court." An American visitor, in reaction to this crustiness, once asked him whether he would feel the same if both partners were of equal strength. "That is a practical impossibility," Freud replied. "There must be inequality, and the superiority of the man is the lesser of two evils."

AN AUSTRIAN TRAGEDY. Of the many theories on why Freud's attractive daughter Anna never married, the most plausible is that she was too strongly attached to her famous father and thus never able to build a personal life of her own. The severe rashes that broke out on the eve of her participation in the Father-Daughter Tennis Tournament at Innsbruck each year clearly reveal some of her inner conflicts. Perhaps Theodor Reik put it best when, in a thinly veiled anecdote, he tells of a young girl who plaintively says to her mother, "You're so lucky. You married Daddy. I have to marry a stranger."

SIGMUND FREUD'S SECRET WISH. According to those who knew him best, Freud was fond of telling the following story on himself. Because his backhand was very weak, he had developed the technique of switching the racket to his left hand—a practice that worked quite well and was particularly effective for hitting lobs that fell precisely on the baseline.* One day a Mr. Mendel, a fellow tennis club member, was asked if he knew Professor Freud.

"Professor Freud?" said Mendel. "I never heard of any such professor."

Mendel was told that Freud was the world-famous founder of the school for understanding the unconscious and a clinical professor at the university.

"That's strange," Mendel replied. "My son-in-law is a professor of anthropology at the university and I know all the professors, but I never heard of Professor Freud. Wait a minute, the name does sound a little familiar . . . is he the guy with the beard who hits those lobs with either hand?"

After recounting this story, Freud would comment wryly: "You see? A prophet is never known in his own country." Nevertheless, beneath all the joking, Freud bashfully confessed that he would gladly trade all his notoriety if he could become good enough to win the Vienna Clay Court Doubles Tournament.

---

* Freud had mastered the switch-hitting technique by emulating his father, who would creep up on butterflies and get them either coming or going. Nevertheless, his lob prowess and his ambidexterity were outstanding features of what was otherwise a mediocre game.

INTEGRATION ON THE COURT. Freud believed that psychoanalysis might founder because it would go down in history as a "Jewish" science. He hated this idea, but didn't know what steps to take because most of the people who were attracted to it were Jewish. Once Freud developed his Tennis Instinct Theory, his worries were over. The happy marriage of Jewish psychoanalysis and a traditional Anglo-Saxon sport provided a certain paradoxical legitimacy to Freud's theory. His concerns were further reduced by the furor that surrounded the invention of "colored" tennis balls. Introducing colored balls into an all-white club created such a tumble that mere anti-Semitism seemed small stuff indeed. The use of yellow balls particularly ("The Yellow Peril," as it was called at the time) was the final straw and put the finishing touches on any naïve Victorian notions that tennis was only a game. As Freud put it, "It is a cause beyond belief."

YOUR HOUR IS UP. Freud staggered his analytical hours to allow for a five-minute break between sessions. As one patient entered the waiting room, the previous patient left through the private entrance. In the interest of confidentiality Freud acted as a sort of traffic policeman, never letting the two meet, and was thus confounded by the strange ethics of changeover on the tennis courts.

It was not long after Freud began studying tennis psychology that he noted the social mores of the Court

Change. When time was up, and one group walked off as another came on, this transition was handled in a variety of ways, each reflecting a different aspect of the unconscious. Sometimes anal-retentive groups bargained for a little more time ("Just a few more points"); the paranoid group would simply glare and finally say, "You're standing on my court"; the compulsive group would haggle ("It's not exactly four o'clock"); the psychopathic group would say, "*Your* watch has the wrong time"; the passive-aggressive group would leave the court without being asked, but would then delay action for ten minutes by amiably chattering and slowly picking up assorted paraphernalia as they sauntered off the court.

Freud soon realized that his investigation into these matters was a defense against his own awkwardness in properly handling the turnover procedure. He recognized that his formal upbringing never equipped him for social situations that demanded the banter, ease and informality of the "court-turnover interaction." One day it occurred to him that there were deeper roots to his surface shyness. "Having the three o'clock group finish up so that I can go on is similar to my sexual impatience," he wrote in *Autobiographical Studies* (1938). "I feel so guilty about my selfish annoyance that I think I am defending against it by being too much of a martyr. In tennis, I am waiting on the sidelines like a gentleman, waiting for the players to get the message and 'get off' already. I wonder how universal my foolish inhibition is."

These insights made Freud aware of how powerful the feelings were that he carried onto the tennis court.

He soon developed a new, aggressive attitude and manner with much more positive results. In tennis, he walked directly to the net post at his assigned time, turned the winch and lowered the net to the ground. To those who could not quite yet grasp what was going on, he reinforced his intentions by standing at the service line with his arms folded provocatively. In matters of sex he simply abstained for the next thirty years and fantasized about his sister-in-law, who lived down the hall.

II. Chronology

Tennis Analysis Papers of Sigmund Freud

The Unconscious Need to Fail (1896)
Aladdin Wasn't Rubbing His Lamp (1897)
Tennis Secrets (1897)
The Prince Racket: Symbol and Symptom (1899)
Sex Is a Cul-de-Sac (1902)
Dissolution of the Oedipus Complex (1903)
Love Is Not a Zero (1903)
Interpretation of Tennis Dreams (1905)
Introductory Lectures on Tennis Psychoanalysis (1906)
The Autoerotic Aspects of Singles (1907)
Approaching Nirvana: Two Hours of Tennis and a Good Cigar (1908)
The Decline of the Killer Instinct (1908)
The Net Is High (1908)
Disguised Tennis Perversions (1909)
Moral Decay in Our Time (1909)
My Kingdom Is Clay (1909)
Masturbatory Fixations and the Western Grip (1910)
Rough or Smooth? (1910)
Sexual Perversions Revealed by the Two-Handed Backhand (1910)
The Agony of Defeat and the Ecstasy of Losing (1911)
The Enemy Within (1912)
Penis Envy and the Prince Racket (1912)
The Primitive Taboo of the Foot Fault (1912)

Untraditional Warm-Up Exercises (1912)
Carnal Passions and the Dink Shot (1913)
Project for the Scientific Study of Tennis (1914)
Resistance to the Lob (1914)
A Child Is Being Eaten (1916)
The Riddle of the Matzoh Ball (1916)
Thoughts for Our Times on a Rainy Afternoon in May (1916)
Adventures in No-Man's Land (1917)
Origin of the Tennis Heimlich Maneuver (1917)
Fellatio and the Short Volley (1923)
Psychopathology of Mixed Doubles (1923)
The Court Is My Couch (1924)
Strange Tennis Symptoms (1924)
The Myth of the Sweet Spot (1925)
Tennis Dream Theory (1925)
On the Sexual Theories of Children (1927)
Begin Each Day with a Smile (1929)
Papers on Metapsychology (1930)
The Ambivalent Character (1931)
Incest Is a Family Affair (1931)
The Foot Fault (1932)
The Traumatic Roots of the Electra Complex (1932)
Flakiness on the Tennis Court, or the Mental Anguish of Dandruff (1933)
Fuzzy Balls and Pubic Hair (1933)
The McHenry Syndrome (1933)
Associations of a Four-Year-Old Child (1934)
Civilized Tennis Morality and Modern Nervousness (1934)
Enjoying Your Mishits: The Power of Negative Thinking (1934)
The Secret Self (1934)
The Body as a Narcissistic Instrument (1935)
Compulsive Tennis Habits (1935)
The Dark Side of the Human Psyche (1935)

The Nightmare of the Canceled Tennis Game: A Study in Obesity, Perversion and Suicide (1935)
The Symbolic Search for the Lost Breast of Childhood (1935)
The Transition from Sexuality (1935)
The Unconscious Code (1935)
Psychological Warfare Between the White Lines (1936)
Tennis Shame and the Anal Character (1936)
Competitive Parapraxes (1937)
Diagnosing Character Types Through Tennis (1937)
Loving an Inanimate Object (1937)
Man's Prehistoric Nature (1937)
Patricide and Losing Service (1937)
The Wish to Regress (1937)
Autobiographical Studies (1938)
Consequences of the Anatomical Distinctions Between the Sexes (1938)
The Fate of Modern Man (1938)
Female Sexual Development (1938)
The Mysterious Fate of the Underhanded Serve (1938)
The Mystery Under the Skirt (1938)
The Reach Should Not Exceed the Grasp (1938)